Church That Works

Church That Works

David Oliver
and
James Thwaites

First published 2001 by Word Publishing, Milton Keynes, UK.
This edition published 2004 by Authentic Lifestyle.

09 08 07 06 05 04 7 6 5 4 3 2

Authentic Lifestyle is an imprint of Authentic Media,
9 Holdom Avenue, Bletchley, Milton Keynes,
Bucks, MK1 1QR, UK.

ISBN 1-86024-447-5

Cover design by Giles Davies
Typeset by WestKey Ltd., Falmouth, Cornwall, England
Print Management by Adare Carwin
Printed and Bound in Denmark by Nørhaven Paperback

Contents

About the Authors

David Oliver is an associate director of the Marketing Guild and senior partner of Insight Marketing. He conducts seminars for business and church leaders in the UK and abroad. He is the author of *Work: Prison or Place of Destiny*? David works with apostolic and prophetic teams and speaks regularly at church events including *Spring Harvest* and *At Work Together*. David can be contacted at Insight Marketing on +44 (0) 870 7877404 – or visit his websites at www.insight-marketing.com and www.yachtsforfun.com

James Thwaites has been in pastoral ministry for over twenty years. He is currently co-pastoring a congregation formed by the joining of Methodist and Pentecostal fellowships. His main work is focused in the health and business spheres, helping to create a culture and momentum for 'church' in those spheres. He is the author of *The Church Beyond the Congregation* and *Renegotiating the Church Contract*. See also www.newlandscape.net

Foreword

Gerald Coates, Pioneer Team Leader

When God was looking for a word to describe his post-Calvary, resurrection community, he rummaged around in the Greek vocabulary. Quite understandably, he could have found words that were directly related to the Temple, the Synagogue or the Jewish community. But he didn't. He used a completely non-religious word, *ekklesia* (translated 'church'). This quite simply refers to a group of people, a congregation (normally political, rarely religious), an identifiable group or a mob. In fact, the mob that congregated and then purposed to stone the apostle Paul was described, correctly, as the *ekklesia*! The idea that it was an unsaved, unredeemed, godless *ekklesia* (church!) that tried to murder Paul is difficult to get our heads around.

The reason for this is that we have made 'church' religious, although the original Greek word *ekklesia* never refers to a building or a religious gathering. Today, when we refer to the church, it is nearly always in terms of what happens in a special building at special times on special days. In fact, being religious is doing 'God things' at 'God times' in 'God places', and rarely elsewhere. The person who reads his or her Bible on Sunday at 6.30 p.m., prays with others at 7.00 p.m., listens to teachings at 7.30 p.m. or gives thanks for the body of Christ and for life itself at 8.00 p.m., but doesn't do it anywhere else – at home, in the workplace, at school or with friends – is, quite frankly, religious!

I have noticed in the last two or three years, even among the New Churches, phraseology slipping into fashion that five or ten years ago we would have laughed at. People talk about 'going to church' or say 'I will see you after church'. It is not unusual to hear people talk about 'going to the service'. As I often quip, 'Services are what we have on motorways, not in church buildings'. In other words, we see ourselves as church when we are gathered, worshipping, praying, listening and responding; but do we think we are equally significant when we are the scattered people of God? Whether deliberately or unintentionally, we empower leaders, meetings and resources, most of which go to maintain this thing that we call 'church'.

Whether you are one of the thousands of young people haemorrhaging from the church at this time or you are a part of the post-Toronto, depressed/pre-revival, disillusioned older generation, it is easy to become cynical and disengaged. David Oliver and James Thwaites suggest another way forward: a way of empowering the individual and groups of people in the fields of education, the arts, the workplace and other areas within our culture.

James and David don't pretend to have the whole picture, so let us not suppose that this book's teaching or emphasis will do everything we want God to do in our location or our nation. But it is a vital contribution to a church where the overwhelming minority do the overwhelming majority of jobs, whether it be preaching, administrating, leading worship or dealing with communications. The culture which surrounds us, and of which we are a part, is heating up at an alarming rate. We have to live in this world not as what we would like it to be but as it is. In other words, we have to come to terms with reality even if we don't like a lot of that reality.

This culture is highly interactive and participatory. When I was a boy, *The $64,000 Question* was one of the top-rated TV shows. The questions got more difficult until the contestant was eventually put into a soundproof box with earphones strapped to their head: isolated, alone, highly nervous and sweating! Witness *Who Wants To Be a Millionaire*: no isolation, no earphones! You can phone a friend or ask the audience for help: it is highly interactive, broadly participatory, and engaging. And that is our culture, this is how people are taught at school, trained in jobs, or retrained. It is the world of the internet, the worldwide web, multi-choice television and flick-of-a-switch radio. It must become the culture of church.

Failure to adjust our models of church, emphasis of ministry and social involvement may make little difference to the church this time next year. But within a decade or so, unless we change, we are bound to become even more irrelevant to the lost communities that surround us. Success will come as we acknowledge our present failure, learn from it, make adjustments and move on. This book may help us do just that.

Dave Richards, Salt and Light Ministries International

Once more, David Oliver and James Thwaites challenge our presuppositions on how we 'do' church and how we value our workers and their callings in Christ. This is not a book to make you feel comfortable, but a book to debate, to be challenged by and, most of all, to pray over to see if Jesus, the head of the church, is awakening us to a different sound.

There is a new alarm clock ringing in my heart! For years, I have envisaged a new way of doing church, where the church supports its workers, not the workers the church. Could these be the first groanings of the birth pangs of a new day in our unfolding history?

Watching the early stages of these new thoughts emerging into practical ministry has been fascinating. We have been wrestling with this in Kenya, Zimbabwe, New Zealand, Sweden, North America and the United Kingdom. Wherever we share these new insights, faith and hope begin to arise within the people of God. The challenge, however, is: can we start to act new, as well as think new? Is it really possible to translate these revelations into a new way of doing church?

Currently I see three things that will affect this challenge. The willingness of church leaders to take up the challenge. The willingness of the workers to understand and accept their workplace callings. The grace of God enabling all of us to hear the voice of the Holy Spirit amongst the current cries and concerns in our world, so we can truly hear and obey what the Spirit is saying to the churches.

As we read this book we should be asking God 'How can we put the truths we see into practical reality?' Wrestle with David's and James's insights, and ask the Spirit of God for revelation, to enable us to do his will and to find an 'administration suitable for our times'.

Introduction
It's Time for Release

David

I woke up sweating in the lakeside log cabin. In my dream, God's voice was saying 'It's time for release. It's time for release!'

Nearly twenty years ago, the message in this book was birthed in very different ways in both authors. During these past two decades, with few exceptions, the church, and in particular its leadership, have seemed for the most part disinterested. In the last three years, however, we have seen a sudden and global explosion of interest. So much so that many pastors are now beginning to sit up and take notice.

From almost nothing, now all kinds of expression of this topic have been getting airtime. I was recently invited for the first time to do sessions on 'The Kingdom of God at work' in the King's Bible College and in Redcliffe College, Gloucester. In 1998, Spring Harvest had their first ever Christian leaders' conference aimed at working leaders and church leaders (Sheffield – *At Work Together*): I was also privileged and excited to be invited to be part of that experience. NFI's Stoneleigh Bible Week featured this topic at their summer event, as did Salt and Light and Pioneer. Power FM in New Zealand and Kenyan Christian

Radio have also featured the material. During the same period, there has been a surge of books all expressing a 'sound from heaven' that is getting stronger and becoming irresistible.

In the past two years, James and I have been invited again and again to talk about church and work in the UK, India, Australia, Sweden, the USA, Zimbabwe and Kenya. It is as if the prophetic word, voiced in its infancy nearly two decades ago, is starting to take hold. The mustard seed of revelation is growing into a tree that will fill the whole earth. In this area of life, it may just be that the Kingdom of God is 'coming of age'.

This book, then, is effectively a sequel to James's *Church Beyond the Congregation* and my *Work – Prison or Place of Destiny?* Our prayer is that it will help answer the many questions from thousands of saints and leaders who have been asking 'What next, then?' and 'Where do we go from here?' This book is not a comfortable read: it challenges beliefs, practices and theology. Its goal is to dig deeper, challenge harder and help saints and leaders alike to be alert and responsive to the prophetic sound that is breaking out through God's church all over the world.

The saints are stirring, and they know God is on the move. Sleeping Beauty has been kissed on the lips and she is very much awake to the new world around her. The time of her destiny is at hand. God has been preparing his wonderful church for just such a time as this – a time for *Church That Works*.

1

I Can't Wait for Monday Morning

David

I don't know who you are, reading this book. Maybe you are feeling great – poised and ready for action. You may be a mum in the home, wondering how to make sense of, and put spiritual value on, what you do. Perhaps you are a student at school, college or university, wondering if there is any point in wasting your time on education that sometimes seems so far from godly purpose and meaning. Perhaps you are a working man or woman, frustrated, complacent or longing for something, almost anything, but not sure what. You may be aware that a new sound is coming from the heavenlies – it's a sound that will break the Christian 'caste' system wide open – a sound for every man, woman and child in the Kingdom of God. A sound that, if we have ears to hear, is getting louder and closer. Wherever you are, with God's help I believe this is for you.

I like to interact with my readers, so could we repeat three lines together:

- God loves work.
- Work is spiritual.
- God wants me to find him at work.

I believe that if you take to heart these truths and live them, you will untether this elusive thing we so often call destiny.

The last words of a dying man

I remember vividly my father's death, and I will never forget the things we talked about in those last days of his life. In the same way, the last words of the New Testament church's first martyr, Stephen, were to have a profound impact. As Rich Marshall points out in his book *God@Work*, Stephen was almost certainly some kind of business administrator and, just before he died, the Holy Spirit anointed him to preach a message summarising God's dealings with our world. The early church would never forget those words, and it is one of the few messages recorded in full in Scripture. It is in these anointed last words of the first martyr that God shows us for all time how he sees history and how much he loves, values and works through men and women in the world of work. He also shows beyond doubt that work is godly, significant and spiritual, that it carries destiny, and that working men and women in God change history. In this message, Stephen focuses on three main characters. I wonder if you can remember who they are. What names are you thinking of right now? The key names in the passage are Abraham, Joseph and Moses.

Abraham is the father of the faith for both Jews and Gentiles – you don't get much more spiritual or significant than that. But he accomplished that role as a travelling farmer, a businessman, a landowner, a cattle rancher and an investor in silver and gold. Every tribe, language, people and nation will one day stand before the throne of God, and it will be because of God's promise to a working man.

Joseph's prophetic ministry began in animal husbandry and took him from there into service in prison management and finally into the highest government office – from where he managed global food supplies at a time of global shortage. His supernatural gifting in the workplace was a key ingredient in the outcome.

Moses was an academic, a nomadic farmer, and managed his father-in-law's flocks before finally becoming a national political leader.

Let us notice a few things in passing

- These men were not official priests, Levites, pastors or church staff.
- They were not paid by the church of the day.
- God used these three working men to change the course of world history for the Jews, the Gentiles and the church.
- In each case, God used their working environment to shape them, and through them – in their place of work – he opened up doors of function and destiny in the Kingdom of God.

I want to say right now that God loves work, God loves me at work and God wants to be working with me at work.

Does God still use the world of work to extend the Kingdom?

In my book *Work – Prison or Place of Destiny?* I looked at twenty-four of God's heroes or models from Scripture who were working men or women. I also referred to at least twelve authors or contributors to Scripture who were working men and women.

In Hebrews chapter 11, which is the chapter on the heroes of the faith, sixteen people out of the seventeen mentioned were working men and women. That should inspire us, liberate us and encourage us.

In the past two decades, the focus of much of the church and most of our resources has been church gatherings, church programmes and church activity. The Bible is not a book centred on the church in gatherings. It is a book about men and women at work, a large part of it written by men and women at work, and written for men and women at work. Let me illustrate.

Over Christmas, my wife Gill pointed out to me something fascinating about the birth of Jesus. How did Almighty God choose to reveal his son's birth? He chose working men and women from both ends of the working system. He sent angels to lowest income agricultural workers – the shepherds. He also sent supernatural revelation to high-income flexitime consultants in the form of the wise men. In the book of Acts alone, God uses a value-added retailer, a paid soldier, a high-end fashion dealer, an international finance minister, a prison warder and two people in manufacturing, together with five apostles who worked in a mixture of part-time and full-time paid employment. This was given to us as the New Testament model for God's way of extending his Kingdom and adding to his church.

If we are not very careful with our theology and the teachers' hermeneutics and exegesis, we will over-spiritualise the Word of God. In our focus on the detail we can miss the whole point. The Bible is not written for theologians, nor is it written primarily for church leaders – it is inspired and written for working men and women in every sphere of their working life.

Daniel – a real example for us in a real world

> Then the king ordered Ashpenaz, chief of his court officials, to bring in some of the Israelites from the royal family and the nobility – young men without any physical defect, handsome, showing aptitude for every kind of learning, well informed, quick to understand, and qualified to serve in the king's palace. He was to teach them the language and literature of the Babylonians [or Chaldeans]. The king assigned them a daily amount of food and wine from the king's table. They were to be trained for three years, and after that they were to enter the king's service. Among these were some from Judah: Daniel, Hananiah, Mishael and Azariah. The chief official gave them new names: to Daniel, the name Belteshazzar; to Hananiah, Shadrach; to Mishael, Meshach; and to Azariah, Abednego. But Daniel resolved not to defile himself with the royal food and wine, and he asked the chief official for permission not to defile himself in this way. Now God had caused the official to show favour and sympathy to Daniel. (Dan. 1: 3–9)

The first thing we learn from Daniel's life is that he wasn't in the ideal environment. It wasn't his choice and, in many ways, it was a sad start. Daniel was taken captive in his teenage years and sent to a foreign land with a foreign language, foreign culture, foreign food and even a foreign name that I suspect he was not keen on! I want to say to us all today – rich or poor, man or woman, slave or free – our upbringing, our background or our status doesn't have to be a barrier to God moving through us. The same is true of our parents' treatment of us or our business success or failure.

Some of us reading this today are missing God's destiny in our lives because we have ruled out his work in us on account of our background, our marriage, our history, our family. Maybe some of you are in a situation – work, home, culture, location – not of your choosing.

In the dark and lonely moments, Daniel could so easily have questioned the will of God. He could have blamed his parents, he could have blamed God and become angry or bitter. He could have chosen despair and helplessness. He could so easily have questioned his ability to fulfil his destiny: 'God, how can I fulfil your destiny for my life in this place – in these circumstances?' But he did not. He knew that his circumstances were not a hindrance to the Kingdom of God, but that rather this was the very place in which the Kingdom was going to be fulfilled and expressed. Daniel was not looking for somewhere else to pursue his full-time ministry. Daniel was not looking for the way out of his family, location, work or cultural circumstances. He actively believed that God was big enough to extend the Kingdom through him, right there.

Daniel understood that God valued his place of work – even though Daniel had no choice in where he was put. Whatever our circumstances, we have the choice of what to believe. One film used this phrase: 'They saw themselves as victims and thus they became the victims'. Whatever our circumstances, family, parents, spouse, children, culture, health – are we seeing ourselves as victims? Because if we are, that is what we will become. If we settle the issue that our home, our study, our place of work is the calling of God, we can reach out positively in faith for anointing. If we see work as spiritual, as our prime place of function and destiny, then let us call on the Holy Spirit and believe that his power, his gifts, his anointing will fill us and our work supernaturally.

What can we learn from Daniel?

Daniel 1:8 tells us that Daniel resolved not to defile himself. That was his starting point, not his conclusion; his beginning and not the sum total, but it served as an important starting point. I have no doubt that God wants his disciples in the workplace and the starting point is 'I will not defile myself.'

Let me share a personal story. Some ten or so years ago I had a dream in which a businessman offered me an investment to start a new company. About a year later, when Gill and I were praying for clarity of business direction, the man came and offered me the business start-up, just as he had in the dream. I had two reservations. Firstly, I had a strong conscience and I wanted to make it clear to the investor that I would not do anything illegal or unethical. I didn't want him investing in me without knowing this and, in my rather clumsy manner, I tried to communicate that fact. Secondly, I really did not believe that his concept would work. I remember saying to him 'I've been your consultant for years – I don't believe this will work.' He responded 'David, you are wrong – trust me, we will make it work.' So nine years ago I started this company with two others, certain in my own mind that it would not work. Today the company turns over $6 million, employs 150 staff and operates in the United Kingdom, the United States and Germany, and has recently attracted a $10.8 million investment to develop its web-based services. The good thing is, God gets the credit – but the starting point for me was a resolve not to defile myself.

How does this example relate to you? I don't know. Perhaps it has to do with money. Perhaps it has to do with friendships or relationships. Perhaps it has to do with cheating or stealing from our employers. Perhaps employers or friends want us to do something that is not right – some shady deal – and that godly resolve needs to be our starting point. When we work, we need to work God's way and not the world's way: honestly rather than dishonestly, straightforwardly rather than convolutedly. It can be hard to be all these things, as it was for Daniel in Babylon. That's why we need God and that's why we need each other, to enable us to stay strong in our faith and wholesome in our actions.

The problem we can have as Christians is that the resolve not to defile ourselves can become an end in itself. We might have a calendar with a scripture on our desk and we might not laugh at dirty jokes – and that can be difficult because they are sometimes very funny! People have learned not to blaspheme around us and we occasionally get to share the Gospel. But there is more. I want you to hear this prophetically: *God has more*.

Daniel's resolve was not a case of hanging on until he found something spiritual. He wasn't holding on in the 'secular' world, waiting to do something spiritual in the church. Something wonderful was being released. His godly resolve to stay pure was like the ignition key turning in the car. It was necessary to start the motor, but it was his faith in the God of work that enabled him to press down on the throttle. It was his expectation in God that put the gear stick in drive, and sent Daniel away on a high-speed drive with destiny: one which was going to impact every area of his working life and produce Scripture in our hands in this chapter 2,600 years later.

Brothers and sisters, the God of Daniel is the same yesterday, today and for ever. That same God loves you, and he loves you in your place of work. That same God wants you and me – every one of us – to walk in his ways and in his good deeds, to discover his works of service every day in the places where we work. The New Testament says that this includes men and women, slaves and free, of any tribe or culture. It doesn't matter where you and I work. God is saying to us today 'Let the chains fall off. Let the clutch go down, let the throttle engage, let the gears click in and let's ride the vehicle of my love, my destiny, my deeds, my works of service – whatever your place of work.' I want to shout Amen!

Every month or so I run a city-wide event, based on my first book *Work – Prison or Place of Destiny*? Let me ask you three questions that we ask during these roadshows. Where is God when we are at work? What is he doing? What are the implications of that? Below this sentence is space for you to write in your answers. Would you do that right now, please?

. . . .

. . . .

. . . .

. . . .

I wish I were sitting with you right now. Your answers would tell me what you really believe. Your answers would tell me what theological viruses you have in your heart and soul. I will be praying for you because I want you to be free: free to work with all the fullness of God available to you; free to hear his affirming, encouraging voice in your workplace; free to love your work with agape love; free to long for Monday morning, because God was there before you left home. His angels and his own presence have been hovering over the desks, the vacuum cleaners, the PCs, the chairs. What is he doing? He is working, speaking, loving, helping, guiding, revealing, organising; doing so much more than we can ever ask or think.

Let me ask another question – is God more real in your Sunday meeting or at work on Monday? The answer depends totally on what we believe. You go to a church gathering expecting to meet with God and so, by and large, you do. Go to work believing his presence is there, that he is waiting for you and wanting you to be the channel to unlock it. Dare to believe it: come on, you know what Daniel believed. When Jesus said 'I will never leave you', he meant never! Being constantly filled with the Spirit means first thing Monday morning and the rest of the week – not just in a one-off Sunday encounter.

My prayer, as you read this, is that God will open your eyes to the wonder, the joy and the liberation of his presence and his purpose in our place of work. If we can see it together, brothers and sisters, faith will start to burn in you and me and we will be desperate to 'get stuck in' on Monday mornings! God loves Monday mornings.

We can even discover a new intimacy with God at work. Where did Adam have his richest place of fellowship with God? It was in the garden. What was the garden? It was his place of work. God loves work and loves us at work so much that he wants to have intimacy with us and meet with us in the workplace. Like the lover in Song of Solomon, God is waiting at our workplaces on Monday morning, longing for a loving intimacy that will engage the workplace, wherever that is for you. When I travel, the thing I long for most is to see my wife when I come home. It stirs something at a very deep level when I see her waiting at the arrivals barrier or opening the door when I arrive home. In some sense, I believe God is waiting for our return into the workplace. Try it tomorrow. Start the day by asking him 'Are you waiting for me at work? Will you be there with me?'

I remember meeting with one client in the Crown Plaza at Heathrow. We were involved in some training and development. We had flown in the evening before from Finland and were due to take a session in personal development and coaching. After my client walked in, within a few words we were prostrate on the carpet of my hotel room, with my client crying out to God from the very depths of his being. This was not the first time I had experienced the heavy, knee-prompting weight of God's presence, but it was the first time it had happened in quite this way. God was there, and the coaching session that day included the sharing of Scriptures, deep personal prayer and some practical suggestions for family as well as business situations. What had happened? I am not really sure, but I have no doubt that the presence of God and his angels was every bit as real as similar encounters we experience at times in a local church gathering.

Women in the home: did you know that you will not find the term 'housewife' in Scripture? You can feel free to change your title. Is it important? Probably, because what you call it is what it becomes. My wife, Gill, is adamant that she is not married to the house, never has been, doesn't want to be and never will be. Proverbs 31 calls you 'household managers'. Feel free to give yourself a business card with your new title on it. One great application of this was modelled by my friends Maureen Church, Janette Coombs, Rose Kenward and others, who for years worked in twos and threes in each other's homes, helping each other manage the household – the church at work in the home.

During your day, you can find intimacy with God. He's there and he wants you to know it – let's reach out and meet him, whenever and wherever we work.

The Favour of God

'Now God had caused the official to show favour and sympathy to Daniel' (Dan. 1:9). Notice that it says God caused it to happen! At work, as in life, there are seasons. It is a struggle and a strain to keep asking God 'What is my destiny?' 'What is my calling?' It is a lot easier to say 'What is God doing where I am?' 'Where do I sense God's favour?' And then we can work with God at what he *is* doing.

I was recently working with a group of young men in their early twenties who were earnestly trying to find God and express their walk with God in a new business venture. We fasted together for a day, determined to hear God together. During the day, we uncovered three unprompted commendations from clients of theirs. One of the clients had a twelve-day contract for their telemarketing services. The boys knew him as 'the whinger'. He rang up while we were together and said he was so delighted with the first three days' work, he was going to pay for all twelve days in advance! In twenty-five years of running my own business that has never happened to me! The cheque came without any prompting. That is the favour of God and it gave us a clear indication that God was with us and that the boys were on track.

As we work in partnership with God, let's expect him to cause things to happen and let's be on the lookout for them. Gill is involved with a parents and toddlers group. A group of ladies led by Lynne Jones had a vision, began to follow the practical implications and suddenly found themselves with the favour of God. Within the first few weeks, they had exceeded their capacity and had a waiting list. God raised the profile, and mums and dads have come. In just a couple of weeks there were 140 individuals.

Not only does God want us to know his presence in the world of our work, he also wants us to experience his divine and eternal purpose through our work. Daniel could never have known the full ramifications of the cosmic purpose God was working through him. This divine purpose became visible as Daniel worked faithfully for God, serving those in authority and keeping away from things that would defile him and bring him down. And so it can be for us.

SAS saints

'To these four young men God gave knowledge and understanding of all kinds of literature and learning. And Daniel could understand visions and dreams of all kinds' (Dan. 1:17). Notice the wonderful blend here of human knowledge and learning with supernatural gifting and manifestation. In your college, university or workplace, God is interested and committed to helping us with research, reading and study. And if we will believe it today and reach out for it today, as we apply ourselves to literature and learning, God will give us knowledge and understanding. Whatever your job today, models of best practice, strategies and insights move at a rapid pace. Here are some examples:

- It used to take 108 men five days to unload a ship: today it takes eight men one day.
- It is believed that within ten years, ninety per cent of white-collar jobs will no longer exist, or will have been reconfigured beyond recognition.
- Value changes – it wasn't that long ago that steel ruled, but in today's values:
    - A computer chip costs $42,000 per lb.

- A silk scarf is $1,900 per lb.
- A Mercedes costs $19 per lb.
- Steel costs 19 cents per lb.

Business strategies used to be revised every two to three years; now it's not uncommon to revise strategy every two to three months. God's people – if they would only see it – are incredibly well equipped for such a task. We have been taught the Word of God, and its principles are firmly rooted in us. We have within us an eternal source of wisdom and understanding and, as we apply ourselves to literature and learning in our fields, God will continually give these to us. He will open our minds and help our memories.

In the UK, we have some crack troops called the SAS. It takes 120 armed soldiers to take out four of our SAS troops and it costs around £1 million to train each SAS member. All the changes exploding around us in the world of work are calling for the crack troops of this generation. I believe that we, the church, have the people and the answers, we have the way forward and we have hope, just as Daniel and his friends did. We really could be the SAS of the working world if we could see and believe in the training we already have. We are the prepared ones. We understand biblical truths – which incidentally work in the world of work – and of all the people on the planet, we are probably the best at implementing these truths in the workplace. Where is the new generation of men and women, young and old, who will serve the Kingdom of God in our state schools? Where is the new generation of godly nurses and doctors who will light up their sphere with the faith? In one of our recent Sunday celebration meetings, we asked for a response from those who were in, or committed to going into, education. Over fifty men and women came forward. As we witnessed this particular response, I thought 'These fifty people could change this country.'

Our company was approached by a manager from KPMG who said 'What we really want to buy is your knowledge.' Brothers and sisters, God is interested in what you read and learn, and wants to supernaturally increase your knowledge and understanding. Fifteen years ago, a friend of mine, Chris Lever, was a PE teacher in a state-run secondary school. He began to believe in God's world of work and began to hear heaven's sound. He dared to believe in the favour of God and dared to believe God could give knowledge and understanding. Today, much to his own surprise, he is programme director at Cranfield – Europe's leading management school. God not only gave him favour, but also gave him knowledge and understanding in all kinds of literature and learning. Chris, from his unlikely beginnings, has written for Cranfield and has trained in Whitehall, at Compaq and with other world-leading companies. God is at work and wants his church at work.

Of course it wasn't just wisdom and knowledge for Daniel, it was also visions and dreams from God – the supernatural at work. I remember travelling for one client, running seminars around the United Kingdom. At the end of the seminar, delegates were asked to sign a standing order for my client's service. At venue after venue, delegates were not signing. I knew the service inside out and knew its integrity and its value. There was no conflict in my mind about its value or about the appropriateness of asking for the standing order. I asked a few intercessors to pray. That night, in my room at the Hilton Hotel in Garforth, Leeds, I had a dream. In the dream, I saw two pages of paper with typed sentences. I woke up quickly and wrote down what I had seen, and the following morning before the session started I asked the conference manager, Barbara, to type it up and put it on an overhead. I used the overheads in my presentation and something like sixty per cent of the companies signed up that morning! When they had all left, I sank to my knees in the Harewood suite and praised God for his faithfulness.

It may not be visions and dreams for all of us – it will be whatever spiritual gifts God has given you to empower you in your place of work. Jesus used these gifts, and for every time he used them in the synagogue (church) meeting context, he used them five to ten times in other areas of life. Whatever your gifts, God has given them to you to use wherever you are and in whatever you are doing.

The end results

'In every matter of wisdom and understanding about which the king questioned them, he found them ten times better than all the magicians and enchanters in his whole kingdom' (Dan. 1:20). Could we dare to believe, as we read this, that God would make us ten times better than all the others? Back in the book of Daniel, something powerful, releasing, hope-inspiring and relevant was being recorded for us to learn from all these years later. This is a pregnant word for our generation of working men and women – that the God of heaven invests in his working people a righteous destiny, wherever they are, whatever their working environment. The God of the Kingdom within us can stir up and release knowledge, understanding and learning of all kinds, and blend that with the supernatural dimension.

This active, faith-filled, believing spirit in Daniel had an incredible impact on him and his colleagues, on the nation and its kings and leaders, and on the international scene. It had cosmic and eternal implications. Many of you will find that these words, or the concepts behind them, resonate in your hearts today. We know this is how it should be and, in the last few years, deep down, we have dared to dream that it really could be like that for us. There is a sense in which every one of us reading this has more than Daniel and his pals had. If Daniel could do it with his pagan boss, with occult practitioners as peers and managers, and without a worldwide move of the Spirit, then maybe, just maybe, we could see the church at work and be the church at work.

It is time to settle the issue. Time is short and our lives are short. Why do I do what I do? Am I in it because it is easy? Am I in it because of the money it makes? Am I in it because years ago God took me there? Am I in it for myself, adding God to what I want to do? Or am I in it because I am confident it is where God has placed me for now? It is time to settle the fact. Your work is not an accident; it is where God has called you and it is where he has placed you.

Whoever we are – working hard in the home; student; factory worker; office worker; medical worker; entrepreneur – are we doing whatever we are doing because we are disciples and this is where he has led us? If that is our primary motivation, we will bring pleasure to God and release his power. If we have settled the issue, if we know we are called of God and if our motives are pure, we can legitimately expect God to anoint us. We can expect him to move and continually see our faith and expectation levels grow.

I want to encourage you to find a place of faith: faith for your job, your home, your study, your projects. I want to encourage you to see work as God sees it: a high calling, valid, valuable and highly spiritual. I want you to have the peace and joy that come with knowing that you are in the centre of God's will. I want to urge, encourage and stir you to find faith at work – daily faith, long-term faith – now. Work is not some kind of stopgap, plugging the hole until full-time ministry or eternity arrives. We have heard it said so many times that without faith it is impossible to please God. Can we find that faith? Can we feel the fresh wind of God blowing hope, anticipation and faith once more?

Let's take hold of faith to believe that the outpouring of his Spirit was not about filling churches with people, but rather about releasing the saints to flow like the Ezekiel river into our homes, hospitals, classrooms, offices, factories, shops, armed forces and consultancies. Faith for you teachers and medics; faith for you students and household managers. Faith to believe that God has actually planned to use you in his purposes. Faith to believe that you are where he has placed you. Faith to break out of any self-imposed prison and see work as God really sees it – a high calling and a pleasure to his heart. Know and believe that you are his church at work – like Daniel – whatever your circumstances, whatever your past or present pain.

2

Where Has the River Gone?

David

Before I answer the question posed by this chapter's title and before I tell you what it means, let me set the scene.

Evangelicals, non-charismatics and charismatics

The language of the river may not scratch your itch, but the sense of it should. Whatever our theological persuasion, it seems to me that we are up against it as far as contemporary church is concerned. Large chunks of our young people are finding church to be irrelevant and boring. 'That's not new,' you will say. True, but the scale of it is. Then, of course, someone else will say 'It's not the church's role to be relevant – in fact relevance can be idolatry.' Maybe, but incompetent and unnecessary irrelevance could be scandalous. If we cause our children to stumble, it could just be the millstone garland around the neck for the church of this generation.

Research done by Mark Greene at London Bible College reveals that 47 per cent of evangelical congregations consider the teaching to be irrelevant to their everyday lives. Furthermore, when they are asked how well it addresses the issues they face, work scores very poorly.

On a scale of 1–4, where 4 = high relevance and 1 = lowest relevance, the scores were:

- work: 1.68
- home: 1.83
- church: 2.12
- personal: 2.57

If that is true, the church is failing to equip us to interact with the world.

In another LBC survey, different age groups were asked to rate the relevance and trustworthiness of the church. Those aged 50+ rated the church as third out of thirteen in relevance and trustworthiness. Those aged under 35 rated the church bottom in relevance and trustworthiness. Contrast that with a MORI pole reported by the Daily Telegraph on 24 March 1999: over half of the men and women aged 16–21 interviewed said that they wanted to run their own business and were planning to be millionaires by the time they were 35. Note the natural focus in this age group on work and their perspective of what success looks like.

In a well-known UK church group, a survey included the following questions and answers:

Score from 1 to 10: 1 = never and 10 = often.

1 How often have you heard a message that has taught work as a high calling or vocation from God? 3.7
2 Do you believe that your pastor or church leaders really see your work as a calling, and spiritual? 5.8
3 How well do you think your local church relates to you in your calling at work? 3.9
4 How relevant are Sunday gatherings to the workplace? 3.8

On 1 March 2001, the Daily Telegraph cited a survey of 17,000 Europeans, one-fifth of whom indicated that they despised the church and had greater confidence in the police and the media. In Britain, 51 per cent said they did not have very much confidence, while 71 per cent declared greater faith in the police. At a time when the police in the UK are at a low in popularity and perceived trustworthiness, this is distressing indeed. Marriage emerged as the most trusted institution in 17 of the 18 European countries surveyed.

The message is here for us – let's read the signs of the times. The working institution of the police and the created institution of marriage score highly, while the church, as it stands and is perceived to stand, is despised by one-fifth!

Recent figures from Canada show that 3.2 million people (10 per cent of the population) were once active churchgoers, but no longer are. Even more shocking is the claim that one million of those have been through YWAM. Why? Somehow the church has failed to be relevant.

So if the church is to be there, if the church is to be relevant, there will have to be some changes in belief, some changes in practice, some changes in attitude. In short, a reformation of ecclesiology.

The journey has begun

Many pastors have begun to affirm more actively and stand with members of their congregations in relation to their work. This is a good move. The challenge is, however, that there are still very few resources, particularly in terms of Ephesians 4 ministry gifts (prophets, pastors, teachers etc), being released to the saints with regard to their work context. Also, when the release becomes too real, in that individuals start to bond more strongly with their work than they do with their church, some leaders, feeling their support base under threat, begin to pull on the 'eccleselastic' band to draw the saints back into the congregational fold. Moreover, much of this release of saints by pastors did not stem from a theological conviction on their part. Rather, it has come from the saints taking initiative and pastors seeing the trend and deciding to catch up. However, if the body of Christ is to enter into all of life and be the salt, light and leaven that Jesus spoke of, we will need a much more decided and strategic release than we have seen to date. The river must get to the sea.

The river

> He asked me, 'Son of man, do you see this?' Then he led me back to the bank of the river. When I arrived there, I saw a great number of trees on each side of the river. He said to me, 'This water flows towards the eastern region and goes down into the Arabah [or the Jordan Valley], where it enters the Sea [that is, the Dead Sea]. When it empties into the Sea, the water there becomes fresh. Swarms of living creatures will live wherever the river flows. There will be large numbers of fish, because this water flows there and makes the salt water fresh; so where the river flows everything will live. Fishermen will stand along the shore; from En Gedi to En Eglaim there will be places for spreading nets. The fish will be of many kinds – like the fish of the Great Sea [that is, the Mediterranean]. But the swamps and marshes will not become fresh; they will be left for salt. Fruit trees of all kinds will grow on both banks of the river. Their leaves will not wither, nor will their fruit fail. Every month they will bear, because the water from the sanctuary flows to them. Their fruit will serve for food and their leaves for healing.' (Ezek. 47:6–12)

Notice some of the key ingredients from these verses:

- Swarms of living creatures – life everywhere; 'everything will live'.
- Large numbers of fish – because the river flows there.
- Fishermen along the shore.
- Places for spreading nets.
- Fish of many kinds.
- Nourishment and healing in abundance.

Many charismatics will immediately identify with this passage of Scripture, relating it to the global outpouring of the Holy Spirit that began around 1994. In response to this outpouring, many churches have for some years held meetings variously termed 'The River of God', 'Times of Refreshing', 'The Father's Blessing' and so on. The general purpose of such gatherings has been to wait on God and ask for more of his Holy Spirit. I have personally benefited from these encounters, but there is an ever-present danger that we will try to contain this sovereign move of God by keeping it where it is. The disciples had a similar problem on the Mount of Transfiguration. Peter's response to the supernatural visitation was to try to build a structure that would contain it in the place where it happened. He was told in no uncertain terms that this was *not* a good thing to do! The reality is that had Peter built his structure, he would have begun the 'First Church of the Transfiguration' and the rest would be history. Peter wanted to see the supernatural visitation as an end, whereas Jesus knew it was an important step on the journey and the journey had to continue. He understood the visitation had its place, but the purposes of God had to move on. In fact, it was when he came down the mountain that Jesus' life and ministry moved into a new dimension of power.

I believe it is true to say that the outward manifestations of this 'River of God' have decreased. There are fewer such gatherings in comparison with previous years. In the minds and often on the lips of charismatics is the question 'Where has the river gone?' David Devenish (New Frontiers) used a phrase that helped me understand the questioning dilemma that many charismatics face. He called it 'Post-Toronto depression and pre-revival disillusionment'. So many of us felt sure that this move of God would bring about great revival, sooner rather than later. We had hoped that this 'river' would be the 'more' that our hearts cried out for, and I believe that in the process we ran the risk of trying to build a mindset or a structure that would contain it.

At some point during the days when I was thinking through these issues, I had a dream. In the dream, I was travelling towards the sea. I could smell that wonderful salty smell and sense that sticky sensation on my skin, just as you would when travelling to a British beach. But we were not quite there. Between where I stood and where I knew the sea to be was a fast-flowing river, incredibly clear and beautiful, full of luxuriant underwater growth. There were underwater plants, the like of which I have not seen in real life. There were wonderful fish – clearly visible – swimming in this magnificent water. And above the river were swarms of insects – life everywhere.

As I looked, I saw that along the banks, all the way to the sea, were houses. Each house had a veranda right next to and overlooking the river. On the verandas were teams of men looking intently at something. The dream zoomed in to one of the houses where I could see on the veranda a team of well-known church leaders from many different church streams. The group was gathered around a large machine, about six feet high and three feet wide, peering intently at it.

I sought to see more clearly what this machine was. As I did I realised that it was a machine capable of stitching leather. The river was driving the machine and there was no human hand involved. I sensed that the leather wineskins were in fact being divinely produced by the river – right at the point in time when the river was about to enter the sea.

I believe that the dream points to a time that is pretty well upon us. The houses all along the river are representative of the various expressions of both the church and the nations. The time for the river to get to the sea is now or very soon. And the inference? Somewhere out of this current move of the river of God a new wineskin will emerge that is fashioned by the process of the river itself. We shall see the hand of God do it. The time to look out for this emerging wineskin is as the river begins to reach the sea.

We are asking 'Where is the river of God?' I don't know, but I don't believe it is where it was. I don't know exactly where it is, but I think it is safe to say, biblically, where it is going. I believe that the new wineskin is going to take us to the sea of the unchurched world. Church meetings and gatherings will not be the primary focus of this wineskin. The church all over the world, right now, is undergoing a new millennium change or reformation. And that reformation will – if we will receive it – turn us inside out, so that we become the church, the called-out ones, the gathered ones in the workplace, whatever and wherever that workplace is, paid and unpaid, in homes, colleges, schools and offices.

So this new wineskin is not about defining how we meet, it's about being the church in all of our life and work in creation. It's about the way we think: think about God, think about what he calls church and think about his world of work. As the title of this book suggests, it is about being the church that works. And that river, by definition, has to go into the working world.

From fishermen to fishers of men

Read how one person – Chris Lever of Teleios – has pioneered this journey and made a transition from the congregation to the sea:

> Thirty years ago, I was walking along a dockside in my home town of Poole, England. I asked the first ferryboat skipper I came to if he would give me a job as a crewmember on his boat. (I loved the sea: I had grown up around it and my dad was a marine commando.) The captain said 'Yes' straight away and hired me – I was amazed.
>
> That was the start of an incredible personal journey. Over the years that followed I had great fun and learned a lot. During the day I worked as a member of the crew on a passenger boat and at night I went fishing. I have never lost the excitement of seeing the cod net or a trawl net pour its contents onto the deck. Fish, a car wheel, even the occasional bomb – you never knew what you would catch, and that was part of the fun of it. Bob, the ferryboat skipper, took me under his wing and trained me. In the process we became close friends. Eventually I took my skipper's licence and took command of my own vessel.
>
> Soon after this I fell in love, got married to Sue and decided that life on the ocean waves was not for us. I trained as a physical education teacher and moved to the concrete town of Basingstoke. It was horrible after being used to the open seas! We planned to stay for eighteen months, and then move back home to Poole.
>
> The trouble started when Sue and I became Christians. Sue was convinced that Basingstoke was the place where God

wanted us to be. I knew she was right, of course, but I disliked the place and felt increasingly trapped in a job that on a good day was fun, but most of the time I hated. I tried to move back, but there were no jobs. After seven years, I quit struggling. I settled the issue along the lines of 'Well I'm here, so God please help me figure out what you want me to do.'

I had started to do some leadership and team training for the church. I began to see how important it was both to hear the taught word and to be trained in its application. Today that sounds obvious to many of us, but then it was radical.

Sixteen years ago, I was asked to provide the training for a church conference. By this time, I had learned to listen to the Bible teachers and try to interpret their messages in the design of the training delivery. The conference was great and on the last evening after the farewell speeches, I went alone into the woods that surrounded the camp. I couldn't sleep. I had a growing sense that God was showing me something. As I walked and prayed, it was as if God showed me how he wanted people to discover his plans for them – who they really were and what they might become in him. In this divine encounter, God revealed to my heart and mind something of what he feels about a person's identity and destiny. What I saw that night blew my mind. It was as if I had been let into a holy place and, in the process, felt the heartbeat of God. He spoke to me that night – almost audibly: 'This is your life-work, to help people discover and keep discovering me, and the plans I have for them.'

He also revealed just how incapable, how ill-prepared and how unable I was to do this and to fulfil my destiny. That broke something in me. I felt that God had shown me something precious, shown me my destiny and, at the same time, shown me that I would not be able to do it. My brain and heart reacted – I was so angry with God. With tears in my eyes, I walked through the woods in the darkest part of the night. A couple of hours went by as I prayed and shouted in frustration at God. How could he be so unfair? It felt almost unkind – cruel even. Then, as I stood looking at the night sky, I saw – literally saw – a throbbing red light from within the clouds. About one-third of the sky pulsated with this light. It was as though I had glimpsed the heartbeat of God. I will never forget it.

Nothing much happened for the next two years, but then I was called for a senior teaching post, just along the coast from Poole. It was all I had dreamed of. The job was perfect for me. We could buy our cottage and I could get my fishing boat. This was it! In the middle of the interview – which was going well – God said to me 'It's yours if you want, but I want you to walk away.' By this time, I was learning to say 'Yes, Sir', so I walked. Apart from my wife Sue, no one understood. Everyone thought I was crazy.

Within two months, I was asked by one of the world's largest corporations to join them on their management team as a senior trainer. This came totally out of the blue – I hadn't looked for it. Digital Equipment Co. (now Compaq) gave me a wonderful apprenticeship. I later went on to establish a pan-European business at the company. After seven years, I was offered a senior business development role with one of the 'big five' consultancies. I left to found Teleios (which is described in more detail in *Work – Prison or Place of Destiny?*).

Today I have the privilege of being a director at one of the world's acclaimed business schools – Cranfield. I work with a great team in Teleios. I travel the world, training and doing consultancy work. I have seen people born again and have been able to have conversations with people at key points in their lives. But I remember, too, where I came from and that I still can't do what God called me to do. That means the reality is that I have to rely on him now more than ever. God's river has clearly taken me to the sea. I am now becoming a fisher of men and women.

Take heart

I wonder what thoughts and emotions Chris's story left you with. I wonder how many noticed the supernatural calling that Chris describes. Many of you readers have had some such experience, and it has been buried under the leaves of discouragement or damaged by faulty teaching in your congregations. Let God's wind of encouragement blow those leaves off right now. Lift your head and believe that he really has called you and will lead you.

Others have never had such an encounter. No problem! Notice how, although Chris had no idea of the journey sixteen years ago, God's hand was guiding, creating and leading all the time. All Chris did was respond to the prompting of God in his working environment. As we move into the next few chapters, trust God to let his will unfold and trust him that, as individuals and as church gatherings, we really can flow into the sea.

3

The Church – Back on Line

James

The move to encourage saints in relation to their ministry in the world of work is not a new thing. Ministers and theologians of note in the Reformation, Puritan and Methodist movements taught that work was a calling from God. Various Catholic orders spoke of its value in the pre-Reformation era. Teaching on the power and purpose of work is of course found right through the Scriptures. In more recent decades, leaders in the charismatic movement have taught the saints that their jobs were Kingdom ministry for God. One would think that with such encouragement over so many years we would have seen a whole lot more Kingdom action in the world of work than we have to date. Of course there are notable exceptions to the rule, but for the most part we have seen little, even diminishing, impact from the teachings of Christ on the world of work. One might well ask why.

Some might say it's because the devil is a powerful devil. Yes, true. However, there needs to be a better reason than this, particularly in view of the work of Christ in overcoming him through the Cross. How about globalisation, the internet, fickle money markets, the pressure to keep ahead financially, the bottom line, the rule of money . . . ? I would have thought that when Jesus said that the very gates of hell would not prevail against his church, he had included factors such as these. So, we need to come up with a better excuse than these. What about teaching – surely we could do with some more of the Word? Yes, to a degree. What about leadership – don't we need better, stronger leaders if we are to overcome? Yes, possibly. The truth is, however, we have had these things in fairly good supply, particularly in the past twenty-five years, and again, not much with regard to the world of work has changed for the good and for the Kingdom. If the church waits for more deep and amazing teaching, or for even stronger visionary leaders to arrive, it will be waiting a very long time before things change.

I believe that if we are going to face the main issue that stands in the way of the Kingdom's impact on our world, we need to look again at the statement uttered by Jesus concerning his church. I mentioned it in passing above, but it bears repeating. Jesus said 'Upon this rock I will build my church; and the gates of Hades will not overpower it' (Mt. 16:18). Let's unpack this key verse. The rock is Peter's confession of Christ as the Son of the living God. So that's understood. The gates of Hades, or hell, must be the powers of the fallen angels opposed to the person, purpose and people of God. Granted. So, what does that leave us with? What remains is the seemingly simple term 'my church'. Could it be that the answer we need, an explanation for the impasse we have reached, has to do with something as basic as the term 'my church'? I believe so.

I believe that there's a reason why the teaching we have had on work has not enabled us to prevail against the gates of hell in business, health, education, government, leisure, the arts and media, not to mention marriage and family. It is because our doctrine or understanding of 'his church' has been severely limited. In a word, it's been defective. Our problem is that we have kept the powerful name 'church' inside the meetings, programmes and buildings of the local (or cell) expression of church. We have kept the name 'church' under the managerial control of pastors and ministers, and have not released it to name and empower the saints in all of their life and work. The work of the saints has been called personal ministry, Kingdom work, vocation, calling and so on, but since the fourth century it has never been fully named with the name 'church'. Without that overcoming name, it has not prevailed against those gates of hell. As a result, we, the saints, have not been able to accomplish what Jesus intended that we should accomplish when he said to each of us 'Let your light shine before men in such a way that they may see your good works, and glorify your Father who is in heaven' (Mt. 5:16). As David has indicated, the focus on the saints in their world of work is increasing. The challenge is that if there is no change to our understanding of what it is to be church, the momentum, as in times past, will gradually diminish and we will find ourselves once again inside the same old version of church trying to make it work.

It's time to revisit that most powerful of names and redefine it for this time. We need to restore the name 'church', investing it again with the meaning, the purpose and the power God intended it to have all along. The Reformation did not change the doctrine of the church. The great revivals of the eighteenth century did not challenge the doctrine of the church. The Pentecostals and their close cousins the charismatics left the doctrine of the church intact. This time, it's time for it to change. We have hit the wall and it's not the devil, it's not the world, and it's not a lack of leadership, teaching or holiness. The wall we have hit is the wall at the back, front and two sides of our local (and, yes, even cell) church.

If we are to see change come, if we are to see fire breathed into our understanding and way of work, if we are to be salt, light and leaven to the world, we need to see a revolution come to our vision of church. If we don't, we will remain inside our buildings, looking out, ever wondering why the world doesn't come in and join us. And inside our meetings we will be taught, led and challenged into cultural oblivion. For years, we have said the church needs to get out and into the world. The time has come. The river Ezekiel saw is moving to the sea and the opportunity is now here for us to move with it. The world of work is before us. The saints are ready. They don't have to get out there – they are already there. The question is, will we give them the name 'church' and equip them to be the church where they live and where they work?

I know there are many issues, questions, concerns and fears that come with such statements. However, before we move to address some of these, and, in particular, before we move to steady the ark of the status quo because of fear of the unknown, let's wade into the issues and the challenges presented here. We often hear preaching from the pulpit about the need for change. However, things cannot change if things remain the same. So let's look at where change in our understanding and way of being church might come from. Our starting point needs to be down there at the roots of the church tree. Where did our way of being church come from? To answer this question we need to engage in a little 'worldviewing'.

Worldviewing

The beginning of change, like most things in life, comes when we are able to see things from a new perspective. It's like getting a pair of prescription glasses for the first time, placing them over our fuzzy sight and being able to focus anew on the everyday things around us. Worldview is the word for this. It's about how we form our picture of the world around us, of our friends and family, our church, our work and even of God himself. In the western world the major influence on our worldview has been a fellow by the name of Plato. No, he wasn't an early church leader, nor was he an Old Testament prophet. He was a fellow from an aristocratic family who lost his position of privilege because of war. He lived in Athens, Greece, five hundred years before Christ was born.

The way of seeing reality that he set up in our western mind or thinking is, to say the least, a problem. It's strange to think that one person who lived so many years ago has had such an effect on the way we perceive reality all these years later. It is different with Jesus, because we have made a choice to call him Lord and follow him. However, when it comes to someone like Plato, who was merely a philosopher and a person we have never met, living our lives according to his ideas is quite a problem. So, what's the deal with Plato?

It's not hard to describe the kind of worldview Plato set up. The word that best describes his way of seeing things is 'divided'. Plato didn't believe that the present world held much in the way of meaning or substance. He said that things like reality, perfection and the ideal were found not in the present life but in a realm or a place removed from creation. This removed place he called the 'spiritual' or 'eternal realm'. In effect, he taught that the eternal realm is real and that the present world is only an illusion. Our mission in life, he said, was to escape the illusion and somehow get to the other realm. Now this sounds a bit like God's plan of salvation, rescuing us from worldliness and sin and taking us to heaven. However, the truth is that although it mimics the salvation plan, it is in fact a world away from God's purpose for our lives.

You have no doubt heard the following words contrasted: sacred/secular, spiritual/natural, heaven/earth, eternity/time. It was Plato who caused us to define things in such a divided way. Ministers do sacred work at church – we do secular work in business. Those who pray are ministering in the spirit – we who work are doing it in the natural. The things done to earn a living are transitory – whereas the things done for God (working in the church, witnessing and charitable work) are eternal in value: and on this divided list could go. Essentially, it means that we in the west, in particular we as Christians in the west, have inherited a divided mind. It is this divided life that ultimately works to cut the church off from the rest of life. Jesus said that a kingdom divided against itself cannot stand. Likewise, a mind divided against itself finds it very hard to stand, because it is unsure just where to plant its feet. Is it in the sacred or in the secular? Is it in the spiritual or in the natural? Is it in this life or in the next one? It's very hard to stand in a divided universe.

Plato's crafty plan

It was Plato's plan to destabilise our lives by dividing them. He did it with a definite agenda in mind. You have probably been in or heard about situations where a person creates a problem and then presents himself as the solution to it. They secretly start trouble so that they will be called on to stop it. Politicians have been known to choose this option, particularly when in a fix. This is what Plato intended when he set up his divided universe. His plan was as follows: you set up a realm that is removed from life and then call it perfect, real, ideal, a must-get-there kind of place. You then tell people that where they live and work is not real, not ideal, not perfect and definitely not where they should be. And then you tell them that you just happen to have what it takes to get them from where they are to where they should be. Sounds like a well-worn sales technique, doesn't it? This ploy worked to make people think that they needed someone wise and powerful, some person or institution, to get them from here to there. While Athens said no to Plato's takeover plan, the early church fathers were much more responsive.

Because they came from a Greek rather than a Hebrew culture, most of the early church leaders embraced Plato's thinking and introduced it into their Christian worldview. This meant that over time people read the Bible more from a Greek than from a Hebrew perspective. True to Plato's agenda, and of course Satan's agenda operating through him, it did not take long for the church to become something separate from the people, something that took charge of the Kingdom process. The 'church as construct' (i.e. the organisational form of church that arises from this way of thinking) has become a mediating institution between the present world and the next, between the natural realm and Plato's removed spiritual realm. This was Plato's plan from the start. He fabricated his divided universe so that the institution of the state, ruled by the likes of himself, could take charge of the masses by promising them access to the 'other' realm. The motto 'divide and conquer' is indeed an apt description of his strategy.

Down through history, Bible teachers have declared the value of work to one degree or another. However, our problem is that despite all this good teaching and good intent, Plato has ensured that the church as an institution remains something separate from the saints. Satan has worked it so that the sacred things will always take priority over the secular. He has divided our mind, our world and our church. He has separated the everyday life and work of the saints from what has become the institution of church. One is natural, the other is spiritual; one is temporal, the other is eternal; one is of earth and the other is of heaven – both are divided and we, the saints, are conquered. So, if that's the problem, is there a solution?

There is a remedy, I believe, to the Greek divide. It's the Hebrew vision of the heavens and the earth given by God in the Scriptures. It alone can heal a divided worldview and unite our vision of creation again. It is with a seamless sight of the heavens and the earth that we can begin to bring together the life and works of every saint under the one banner named 'his church'. It's hardly surprising that those in charge of the gates of hell have been so in favour of the Greek divide and so opposed to the Hebrew vision. Let's get ourselves a Hebrew vision and, as one body, the church, face those gates and work to overcome them in line with Jesus' declaration and desire.

4

Seamless Church Under a Hebrew Heaven

James

The church is designed for the world. It was created to reach, light, leaven and salt the earth. It follows from this that if the church has the wrong worldview, it won't be able to fit in relation to the world. If the church is disconnected from the very world it is meant to reach, it's hardly surprising that every attempt it makes to light the world falls so far short. It is from a Hebrew vantage point that we are able to see the church as Jesus intended us to. Developing a Hebrew vision is not as hard as one might think. It is not as if you have to do an intense course in philosophy. Of course, there's a challenge to seeing in line with the Hebrew vision because of the way Plato has blurred our sight. However, what we need to realise is that God designed us to see in line with the Hebrew, and not the Platonic, worldview. This means that the Hebrew way of seeing comes naturally to us. It's important to keep this in mind as we proceed. For if we believe that we are trying to change our thinking into something entirely different, we are more likely to stress out and give up. Remember, that was a part of Plato's trick, to make you think you have to get somewhere else, somewhere you are not, if you are to arrive. It is important that we see this journey of change as a journey into more of who we already are: one that gives us a clearer understanding of what our world really is. Jesus said that if you believe that you already have the things God desires to give, they are yours.

Quite simply, but very profoundly, the Hebrew vision is best explained by the word 'unified'. Remember, Plato's world-vision was marked by the word 'divided'. In contrast to this, the Hebrew worldview is unified: it's one; it's seamless. There is no sacred and secular divide; there is no spiritual and natural split; there is no dislocation between the heaven and the earth.

Let's begin the unification process by looking at heaven and earth. God taught Hebrews like Peter, Paul, Isaiah and Jeremiah that the throne of God, heaven itself, was situated over and above all of their life and work on earth. When any one of them walked out of their house to go into the city to do business, they knew that the very heaven of God was overhead. Heaven was placed over the earth by God to express his rule over creation. God doesn't need heaven for his own sake – he created it for us. He made it to be the crown, the arrival point for our lives in the present age. That's why he put it over and above us in real space and actual time.

This heaven was not visible to the physical eye, but it was very much present and accounted for in the day-to-day life of the Hebrew people. The truth is that most things of power and substance in life are not visible to the eye. Have you ever seen friendship, love, faith or trust? You have, of course, seen people who expressed these things, but the things themselves remain invisible. So, too, with the heaven of God: it is unseen but is expressed and felt through the things that God has made. You can read more about this in Psalm 19.

Under the influence of Plato, most Bible teachers of today say that this heaven-over-earth thing is only a metaphor – which is another way of saying that it's not true. However, God never gave permission to teachers to remove his heaven from over his earth and consign it to some spiritual realm attached to the next life. Paul says in Colossians 1:23, that he proclaimed the Gospel 'in all creation under heaven'. Elsewhere he spoke of a man who was 'caught up to the third heaven' (2 Cor. 12:2). 'Three heavens,' you might say: 'well, now things are getting really complex!'

These three heavens speak of the realms or orders of creation. The first is inhabited by humanity, the second by angels, and the third by the throne of God. These all interrelate and join to set the unified and big picture for our worldview. Plato hijacked the third heaven from over and above the present earth and consigned it to a realm removed from this life. It's time that we put it back. We need to bring heaven and earth together, and let no man, no teacher, no philosopher separate them again in our thinking.

The final point we will cover here regarding the Hebrew worldview relates to the spiritual/natural divide brought in by Plato. For the Hebrews, the spiritual was not something distinct from the natural realm. Rather, the spiritual, or what they called the unseen realm, was one with every created thing. We read about this in Romans 1:20. Paul says here that 'since the creation of the world his [God's] invisible attributes, his eternal power and divine nature, have been clearly seen, being understood through what has been made'. As I mentioned before, the most important things on earth are invisible but are experienced through the things and people we relate to each day.

Here we learn that the qualities, the good and the value in things are in fact expressions of the very attributes, nature and power of God himself. From the created earth through to the glory of his created heaven, God has hidden something of himself in everything he has made. For the Hebrew, things like love, trust and friendship are spiritual qualities that reflect the person of God. These join with other spiritual activities like prayer, worship and service to make up the full composite of our lives in God. For the Hebrew, and for each one of us, all of life is created as spiritual – not just certain sacred or moral parts of it.

Some might feel that this is scary thinking, in that it might sound to them like a New Age-type perspective. However, contrary to the teachings of pantheistic philosophy, the God of the Hebrews was not all things, and all things were not God. Rather, God the Father was and is, as Ephesians 4:6 says, 'over all [things in heaven] and through all [things] and in all [things]'. God is not scared to be found – as Romans 1:20 and Ephesians 4:6 tell us – in and through the things that he has made. If you want to look into this subject further, the book *The Church Beyond the Congregation* examines it in far more detail. Here, I am sketching an outline of the Hebrew worldview and contrasting it with Plato's way of seeing things. As we shall see, these two ways of seeing the world produce two very different visions or understandings of the church.

In summary, the Hebrew vision sees the heaven of God over the earth and the spiritual realm as one with the created realm. It does not divide the spiritual from the natural realm, nor does it dislocate the heaven from the earth. Rather, it brings them into a unified relationship with each other. It is into this seamless vision of creation that we can now place the church that Jesus came to establish in this world of his. What does the church look like under a Hebrew sky?

The church of best fit

The book of Ephesians is often called 'the book of the church'. The reason for this is that teaching about the church figures more in this epistle than in any other. So it follows that if we want to look with Hebrew vision at the church we would go there. We start in chapter 4, where Paul is about to release information regarding the big five – apostles, prophets, evangelists, pastors and teachers. Before he does this, he wants to tell us the reason why God wanted these ministry gifts to be given. What Paul says can only be understood in line with the Hebrew vision of creation. Under any other operating system or worldview it would not make any sense. Speaking of Jesus Christ, Paul says in Ephesians 4:9–10 'Now this expression, "he ascended" [went up], what does it mean except that he also had descended into the lower parts of the earth [into sheol and death]? He who descended is himself also he who ascended far above all the heavens, so that he might fill all things.'

Quite simply, Jesus came down from the third heaven (the throne of God) to the first heaven (the earth). There he lived and died and rose again 'through the heavens' (note the plural here) to take his seat at the right hand of God the Father in the third heaven. You can see how simple this description is and, again, how much sense it makes from a Hebrew perspective.

At the end of his description of the journey of incarnation, death and resurrection, Paul tells us the reason why Jesus did all of this. He said that Christ's purpose in coming from heaven and then returning there was so that 'he might fill all things'. In the context it is clear that the 'all things' being spoken of here are the 'all things' of the present creation. So how is Jesus going to fill all things? To find this out we need to turn back to chapter 1 of Ephesians. It is there that we discover, with our Hebrew vision, what the church looks like and where it's meant to stand in relation to this world.

As we have seen, Plato's vision of creation has powerfully influenced our understanding of church. Because of the Platonic divide, the church as an institution has become something separate from the life of the saints. In accordance with its view of where heaven and the spiritual realm are located, the church tends to travel in a direction away from creation rather than towards it. The church as construct sits halfway between the present world and the age to come as a kind of mediator between the ages. As such, it also stands as the main mediator in the relationship between the saints and their God. It is important to keep these things in mind as we proceed to describe the church that Jesus came to build.

Paul prays the most remarkable prayer for each of us in chapter 1 of Ephesians. His prayer rose out of the depth of his understanding, vision and passion for what he knew to be the church. Again, what he says only makes sense if we take the Hebrew vision of the heavens and the earth seriously. Paul wants us to know the power that God 'brought about in Christ, when he raised him from the dead and seated him at his right hand in the heavenly places'. This place in the third heaven, he goes on to say, is 'far above all rule and authority and power and dominion, and every name that is named, not only in this age but also in the one to come'. He then climaxes his declaration by telling us that God 'put all things in subjection under his [Jesus Christ's] feet, and gave him as head over all things to the church, which is his body, the fullness of him who fills all in all' (1:20–23). Let's unpack this.

Scripture says that heaven has always been God's throne and that earth was made to be his footstool

(Is. 66:1). When God became man his feet touched the earth, and as the man Jesus Christ he was given dominion over that earth. That is why this verse says that all things are now in subjection under Jesus' feet. From death he rose to life and kept rising, ascending through the heavens to the right hand of God. In that place in the third heaven he is now head over all things. He has dominion over both the angelic and human realms under him. From this ascended place all that Jesus is and all that he has won has been given to his body, the church. And where is this body to be found?

Again, let's keep this very simple and Hebrew. If Christ's feet are established on the earth and his head is in the third of the heavens over that earth, then it stands to reason that his body can only exist between his feet and his head. And so it does! Christ's body, the church, stands in Christ right through the created order. Its calling is to draw out and establish the fullness of all things in creation. It stands on earth and is called to grow up through creation to the heaven of God. Its calling is to be the fullness of all that Jesus has filled. It has the mandate and the privilege to complete and accomplish Jesus' desire, expressed by Paul in chapter 4, to 'fill all things'.

What we conclude from this teaching of Scripture is that the church is the people of God living and working in every sphere of creation, called to draw out the good, the substance, the very attributes, nature and power of God in every created thing. The way in which the body fills creation is taught throughout the remainder of the book of Ephesians. We are called, as Jew and Gentile, to join as one new man in Christ. As saints we are called to live a life of love (5:2) and purity (5:3) and are privileged to grow up in Christ (4:15) to the heavens (6:12) in and through the creation spheres of marriage (5:21–33), family (6:1–4) and work (6:5–9).

The extent to which God's strategy for the church comes on line when we apply a Hebrew frame of reference to our reading of Scripture is amazing. The role of ministry gifts, the place of the gathering, the purpose of our working life and more become so much clearer when we place 'the church' in a creation, rather than a congregation, context. Teaching that calls us to 'grow up in all aspects' (4:15) of the creation, 'to the measure of the stature which belongs to the fullness of Christ' (4:13), can be properly understood once we set the right context in place. So, once again, what and where is the church? The church is the body of Christ standing in marriage, in family and in every sphere of creation engaged by our work. The church is called to fill up and fill out every one of those spheres by releasing the light of the divine attributes, nature and power God has placed in each one. Let's now place Christ's body, the church, into a graphic of the Hebrew vision of creation.

Which is the centre and which is the servant?

Once this creation-encompassing vision of the church is established, we can better understand and place the church gathered. In 1 Timothy 3:15 we read that the church gathered, the household of God, is called to be the 'pillar and support of the truth'. Again, if we interpret this phrase in line with our current doctrine of church, we would think this meant that the gathered church was central. Now that we have the big picture in place, however, we can look again and see differently. If the church is the pillar and support of the truth, then what is truth? Scripture says that Jesus is the truth (Jn. 14:6) and that truth is in Jesus (Eph. 4:21). And where is Jesus? Paul tells us in Ephesians that the Son of God stands right through the created order in and through the saints' life in marriage, family and work. It follows from this that the church gathered must be called to be a pillar and a support to the church that exists in marriage, family and work. The pillar is made to support, not to be the centre.

In effect, what this does is turn things the other way around. We have been accustomed to a situation where the people of God serve the church – as meeting and organisation – so that 'it' can do the works of ministry and thereby see the Kingdom grow. Most of the resources have been drawn into the household gathering to try and get it to fill the creation through its meetings, its leaders and its programmes. Scripture, read with Hebrew sight, does not lend support to this strategy. The 'church gathered', in whatever form and in whatever place, is meant to focus on, serve and resource the church in marriage, family and work. The church gathered is called to be the servant of the church as the 'fullness of him who fills all in all'. What we have made the centre is not the centre. The centre is to be found in the life and work of every son and every daughter standing in Christ in creation. The resources of ministry gift, sacrament and word, the name 'church' and more are meant to be dispersed out there to equip the saints to engage and gather their inheritance in creation. These saints are the church. They alone can fill creation through their life and work in the spheres of creation. The church as construct, the church as separate, the church as meeting, cannot and will never fill creation. God never called it to, and the fact is that it is impossible for it ever to accomplish such a feat.

Much has been made of the word *ekklesia* (church) in defining the church primarily as meetings in a building or in a home. The word speaks to us of a called-out people. It was used in Bible times to describe an assembly of a political nature. What has happened is that our theology of church has caused us to emphasise this gathering aspect over every other implication the word *ekklesia* might contain. For example, in Ephesians the word *ekklesia* is never used in relation to the gathering; it is used to speak of a body of people who have been 'called . . . out of darkness into his marvellous light' (1 Pet. 2:9). We have been called out of darkness to be in Christ, to gather in him as he stands in creation and seeks to fill all things. Certainly, the household gatherings of the saints are gatherings of the church, but we need to understand that it is not the gathering that makes them the church. They are the church and so when they gather they gather as that church.

This does not mean that our gatherings are unimportant. The reason why our meetings are failing us, in so many people's estimation, is because of the pressure on them to perform the impossible. They were never meant to be the front line of the Kingdom strategy. We need to see a culture emerge where the 'church as fullness' (from Eph. 1:23) and the church gathered come into right relationship with each other. As this emerges we will, I believe, see the richness, diversity and substance return to the meetings we are trying so hard to keep radical and relevant. Once we break out of the Platonic worldview and see the church as it is meant to be seen, we can begin to bring all of our works in all of life back on line as central to the Kingdom purpose. We, as saints, are the church: our work is the work of the church; our work is on the front line of engagement with the gates of hell. Our work is not secular and temporal – it is sacred and eternal.

We have hit the wall in so many areas as the church. We are not shining anything like the light we need to overcome the darkness. We are not salting the earth; we are being trodden underfoot by the social and economic systems of fallen humanity. We are not leavening the lump that is our world; we are growing stale inside our church buildings and our church meetings. God, by his Spirit, has been stirring up the wells of the eternal within his sons and daughters in these past years. He has been moving to refresh and revive a church that has grown tired. He is raising up people to declare the power and place of all of the saints' work in life. Alongside this, he is bringing into focus the things that have held us back from seeing his church as we should. He is giving us an opportunity to look again and see his church as he intended it to be seen. He is releasing the name 'church' from the buildings, the meetings and the programmes that have held it to themselves, and he is liberating it to name all of the life and all of the works of the saints. Let's take the name 'church' and be the body of Christ, the fullness of him who fills all in all. We'll now take a look at the nature and purpose of these good works of the saints.

5

Church at Work

David

I bet you have had a few viruses on your PC – I have! My heart still pounds when I get an email and the McAfee virus protector alerts me to a danger in the system. I had one recently – a friend's business emailed me with a virus that had wiped out his entire system and sent itself to everyone in his address book. He alerted me before any damage was done, enabling me to delete the rogue email in time. In one of my offices last month we had a virus that took down our entire computer network, lost us data and disabled our effectiveness. We had to wipe out all our old infected data and reload with clean data.

As God starts to move across this planet with a new ecclesiology (doctrine of church), we are going to discover that most of us have an embedded virus in our worldview. This viral serpent will have to be untwined and called out – deleted – and the right information loaded in. I am sorry about this, because I know some of you will have read the word 'worldview' and groaned 'Do I really have to do this chapter? Do I really need a worldview?' The fact is, you already have one: it is already either liberating or trapping you. The distressing likelihood is that it is contaminated by an insidious virus.

A conflict of worldviews

What is a worldview? It is like the foundation and framework on which we build the fabric of our lives. As I write this, I'm looking out over Watership Down behind our home, and in the distance are two large agricultural barns. They were built on a solid, deep foundation with carefully determined, calculated and measured steel frames on which the whole structure hangs. The structure hangs on the framework and bears down on the foundation. Our worldview is just like that. It will take the whole weight of our life and the decisions we make. All the activities we engage in must hang on its frame. Skimp or cheat on the foundations and miss the frame and you have a deformed, disabled, ineffective and misshapen life. You might not see it, but it will surely be evident. Ultimately, we live out what we really believe. That is the only way we can live. In summary: our worldview is the story by which we interpret life and come to our own understanding of the answers to life's key questions. Over many centuries there has been a conflict of worldviews in the church.

Augustine forwards the virus

In Chapter 3 we looked at the influence of the Greek worldview and, in particular, Plato's part in forming much of our western way of thinking. We saw how the influence of Plato's divided world carried on and infected many of the early church fathers. The virus of Plato has mutated in many ways, but its basic DNA – to divide and conquer – is present wherever it goes. As with many infections, it's more likely to be friends and loved ones you get it from than your enemies. Whether you have developed your worldview or not, the virus is already in it and it is likely to have come from your best friend in the church. Take our good friend Augustine, for example. In Augustine's worldview, business was an encumbrance and spiritual contemplation a higher activity. Somewhere he said 'If no one lays this burden upon us we should give ourselves up to leisure, to the perception and contemplation of truth.' This became known as the *vita contemplatio*.

Notice the sinister use of words like 'burden' and 'encumbrance' to describe the world of work. What did those words do to you when you read them? I hope they made you angry, because if they did, your virus detector has just been upgraded. You know now that the virus is there, and you may just get to it before it corrupts the hard drive of your mind. If you felt nothing, may God help you – you may well be infected big-time. What do you feel now as I remind you that he said 'contemplation is a higher thing'? What does that make you feel about your world of work? The inference to be drawn from Augustine's words is that you might just as well give up as soon as you can and spend your life in contemplation. If you do, then God will be more pleased with you and you will become more spiritual. If we see this stuff and do nothing, we continue to allow the slippery scales to slither their way through our souls. From Augustine and other sources such as Plato it is possible to have a virally contaminated theology. Let me highlight a few areas:

- A flawed theology of creation in which we believe that work is somehow part of the Fall and came with the curse.
- The flaw of Pietism, which interprets Scripture as a mandate to separate ourselves. Scriptures like 'Come out from among them' are often quoted, to teach a lifestyle of separation from the world.

- A flawed theology of the church, believing that the church is synonymous with *gathering* or *the meeting*; that when we are not gathered we are not truly or effectively the church.
- A flawed approach to outreach, with a primary emphasis on neighbourhood, which in this stress-filled millennium will only be effective for the few.
- A flawed approach to ministry. This has produced what we could safely call the Christian 'caste system', where all Christians are equal, but 'full-time' Christians are more equal than others! The most damaging and vulgar expression of this caste system is the persistent use of the phrase 'full-time' to describe the upper or ruling class.

The phrase 'full time' is used only once in the entire Scriptures – Romans 13:6. Here it refers to a local government employee in the Inland Revenue, who is also referred to as God's servant. If we persist in using the phrase, we deliberately demean 95 per cent or more of the church who are not 'full-time' and never can be. Many of my closest friends are paid by the church, and they are among the most supportive in the drive to be rid of the phrase. Why? Because it produces a two-tier Christianity, where those not paid by the church can never feel fully affirmed or released to do what they have been led to do. They will always feel second-best, second-rate and less spiritual. God forbid! Think through the following questions with me now, particularly if you are in so-called full-time ministry:

- Are 'full-time' church workers unique in having some special value?
- Are they unique in having uncluttered lives so they can be more devoted to extending the Kingdom?

- Are they unique in having some kind of supernatural calling?
- Are they unique because they can give more time to the Word and prayer?
- Are they unique in living by faith?
- Do full-time workers do more for God than those not in that position?
- Does God put a higher value on Isaiah than on Amos? A higher value on Simon Peter than on Simon the Tanner? A higher value on Elisha than on Daniel?

An instant virus check – right now

As long as this powerful virus has traces in our bloodstream it will affect how we feel about ourselves and about the value of what we do, and it will give us a false perspective of the church. Full-time or any other form of work in the local church is not more spiritual. It is not more highly valued by God. The congregation is not the central player in God's Kingdom, nor, for that matter, is the workplace. Both, along with family, marriage and community, have vital parts to play in its realisation.

Is this virus in my bloodstream or in my church's bloodstream? Here are some questions to check it out:

- Do I or others use the phrase 'full-time' when talking about church staff?
- Do I hear the phrase and do nothing about it?
- Do I or others refer to work as 'secular employment'?
- Do I consider work to be a bit of a bind? Would I rather be doing something more 'valuable', 'worthwhile' or 'significant'?
- Do I believe that ministry from the local church is, in truth, more spiritual than my housework, my office work or my manual work?

- Do I believe that God's call and destiny are a higher thing than my work could be?
- Do I work primarily because it is a biblical obligation?
- Do I regard work as the means to support my family, while I get on with the important bit in the church congregation?
- Do I work for the money, because I believe that I can give more to God and his Kingdom?

If your answer to any one of those questions is 'yes', there is a stronghold to be broken, a mindset to be changed. That mindset has to do with how we view God himself, and how we view his church and his world.

If you and I are called to what we do, there is nothing more spiritual, nothing more wonderful. When we see this, the last traces of Plato's sleeping drug will evaporate, a trumpet will sound in heaven and a patiently waiting and infinitely creative God will be able to lavish so much more of his Spirit, his wisdom, his counsel and his gifts on his people. Mike Pusey, a well-known pastor in the UK, read some of this material in the New Frontiers International magazine. He wrote to me subsequently and said this: 'There was a time when some of us were involved in removing the best men in business to become 'full-time' ministers in the church. Sometimes that was right in God but, looking back, more often than not I don't believe that it was.'

The enemy has taught God's people to view work as secular. I hear the term used so often; it does us no service. The enemy has taught the church to view work as less spiritual, second-best to local or cell church activity. It's a lie and it's time to purge the drug from our system. The issue is not about whether what I do is 'sacred' or 'secular'. The issue is this: 'Is what I do done in the flesh or in the Spirit?' That question, by the way, is equally valid for those paid by the congregation and those paid by their labours in a different sphere.

Call it secular long enough, which we have, and that is what it will become – and it has. When we view work as secular, it has profound implications. Why? It takes meaning, value and a sense of calling away from what we do. It will cripple faith. It will cause the will, the works and the power of God to evaporate.

The concept of secular work cannot be found in the pages of Scripture, and for a very good reason: it does not exist in the mind, the will or the purpose of God. He wants this generation to reclaim the world of work and see his Kingdom come in that sphere of creation – practically, genuinely and excitingly. It is he who wants his church to be the church at work. So let's now discover how the King of the Kingdom sees work itself.

6

Work From Heaven

David

Today's society seems to place a higher value on paid work than on unpaid work. The role of men and women in the home is probably the most underrated, least appreciated and lowest-paid job in the western world. The term 'work', as used in the Bible, cannot be restricted to only that which provides an income. The various Hebrew and Greek words used indicate a deed, an act, doing, making. So we can safely say that work is any expenditure of physical or mental effort. It includes study, manual labour, agricultural work and all other forms of white-collar, blue-collar and T-shirt-clad work. It will include mental and physical, manual and cerebral. Cooking, washing and car repairs are all part of the world of work.

The *raison d'être* for work

- Work is not there to provide a tithe for the church.
- Work is not there to provide God with money that he would otherwise be short of.
- Work is not there to be 'tent-making', to enable me to fulfil my 'ministry'.
- Work is not there for our prosperity.

- Work is not there for our personal fulfilment.
- Work is not there to train us for leadership.

Work may indeed provide some of these elements, but they are fruits, they are not the root or the *raison d'être*. The *raison d'être* is simply that God works and we are created in his image to do likewise. Most of us will express the destiny, the high calling of God, primarily through work. If we will believe this – if our faith will rise to it – then the dynamic of God's Kingdom, the Holy Spirit, will be available, with infinite power and infinite creativity, to make his impact through us in our sphere of work.

As we work, we come to know what it means to be created in God's image. Through our work, we draw out the fullness of all that God has placed in us and in his creation. In and through our work we come to know God the creator – progressively drawing closer to him as we press into his power, presence and purpose in every facet of life.

Work enables us to serve others and thereby contribute to community life. God is a Holy Trinity of sacrificial love, total openness and complete trust. I heard it said in one of the Spring Harvest seminars: 'Other people do not threaten me – they complete me. I become truly free when I open my life for others and share it with them, and when others respond likewise. Then the other person is no longer a limitation on my freedom, but the completion of it.' Work is the primary place where I will apply that fact.

God works

God works! The very first verse in the Bible says 'In the beginning God created [worked at] the heavens and the earth.' Then Genesis 2:3: 'And God blessed the seventh day and made it holy, because on it he rested from all the work of creating that he had done'. In the Genesis description of the creation, God is recorded as one who *makes, forms, builds* and *plants*. These are all words used elsewhere in Scripture to describe work.

While God's work can be distinguished from our own by the fact that he is all-powerful and his work is perfect, his creation work did involve many of the functions we consider work to have:

- He makes things – as a craftsman might.
- He categorises and names things – as a scientist might.
- He plans carefully – one process following another.
- He examines the quality of his work – quality control.
- He clearly defines each component's function – as an engineer might.
- He clearly defines humanity's role and provides resources – as a good manager might.
- His work reflects who he is – as we would like ours to do.
- He takes pleasure in his work – a job well done – satisfied.

Right through the Bible, God is represented as constantly working – ordering circumstances to change our lives, getting involved in nations and in individuals. God is at work – ruling, delegating and providing. In Philippians 2:13 Paul says 'For it is God who *works* in you both to will and to do for his good pleasure' (NKJV). Both his will and his *work* are his good pleasure.

Notice, too, that there is absolutely no distinction between the natural and the spiritual, God creating or God working by his Spirit. From the very first chapter in the Bible, we get the clearest indication that true spiritual activity and work are synonymous. Genesis 1:2 tells us that 'the Spirit of God was hovering over the face of the waters' (NKJV), ready and waiting to create. God was working in the creation, and working by his Holy Spirit. You can't get more spiritual than the Holy Spirit, and the Holy Spirit works!

In Exodus chapter 35 we find one of the first recorded instances of God choosing men and putting his Holy Spirit on them. What for – to act as priests or congregational leaders? No! In verses 31–35, talking about a man named Bezalel and his friends, it says:

> He has filled him with the Spirit of God, in wisdom and understanding, in knowledge and all manner of workmanship, to design artistic works, to work in gold and silver and bronze, in cutting jewels for setting, in carving wood, and to work in all manner of artistic workmanship. And he has put in his heart the ability to teach, in him and Aholiab the son of Ahisamach, of the tribe of Dan. He has filled them with skill to do all manner of work of the engraver and the designer and the tapestry maker, in blue, purple, and scarlet thread, and fine linen, and of the weaver – those who do every work and those who design artistic works. (NKJV)

They were filled with the Holy Spirit for excellence in various work-based skills. And, by the way, the first ministry gift in a work-based setting – teaching – is spoken of here. Work was the first responsibility given to man. Before God gave Adam his wife and family, he gave him work. The Lord took the man and put him into the garden to *work* it and to take care of it. Adam was not so much placed on the planet to worship: he was placed here to work. Eve was created because no helper or counterpart was found for Adam to share in that work.

Work is not the result of the Fall. Work was there before the Fall. It was part of God's personality and integral to his faultless design. Work was to be part of Adam's richest fellowship with his Maker. The Fall tainted work, and brought thorns to the rose bush and weeds to the flower displays. But the rose and the flowerbed were there before and are still there now. Men and women together, from the very beginning, were created to have fellowship with each other and with God by working on his planet, serving each other and serving God in the process.

The thought of work evokes poetry from the very heart of God. In Psalm 104, the psalmist is describing the wonders of creation in poetry set to music. One of these wonders of creation is expressed in verse 23, where it says 'Man goes out to his work and to his labour until the evening.' The psalmist goes on, singing out in verse 31 'May the glory of the Lord endure forever; may the Lord rejoice in his works', here referring, along with several other dimensions of the creation, to the glory of God expressed in and through human work.

Read Psalms 103 and 104 sometime. Both psalms resonate with God's intimate care for and practical commitment to animals, merchants in ships, farming, the wine trade, baking, and so on. There is glory in our work. God made us in his image so that we can fulfil his purpose in ourselves and in the world by working.

God's view of the world

'God created man in his own image, in the image of God he created him; male and female he created them' (Gen. 1:27). The Lord God took the man and put him in the Garden of Eden to work it and take care of it. In Genesis 1:28 it says 'Then God blessed them, and God said to them, "Be fruitful and multiply; fill the earth and subdue it."' (NKJV) God made our human race to fill and care for the earth. It is how and why we were made. It is built into who we are. If we do not work on our planet we contradict our very reason for existence.

How do these early chapters of Scripture describe the outworking of God's plan? Surprise, surprise – it is through the world of work. As we saw in chapter one of this book, from the very beginning men and women in the working world have served his purposes in their places of work. In Genesis we see the beginnings of cities (places of trade and commerce); we see the emergence of farming, herding and nomadic life; we see the origins of music and metalwork.

These shapers of history related their destiny to their working world. And so, it seems, did God. When we read that 'They will beat their swords into ploughshares and their spears into pruning hooks' (Mich. 4:3), we should ask ourselves 'What does this reveal?' It shows clearly that not only do we see weapons decommissioned but also, out of their molten newness, we see newly-fashioned implements of work emerge. We are made to work in the image of a God who works, and for a Kingdom whose King loves work.

Adam and work

- Adam had three part-time jobs, so he was quite busy.
- Adam was given the job of tending the garden that God had planted.
- Adam's second job was to be a security guard – 'The Lord God took the man and put him in the Garden of Eden to work it and take care of it' (Gen. 2:15).
- Adam's third job was to be a zoologist – 'He [God] brought them [the animals] to the man to see what he would name them' (Gen. 2:19).

As we saw earlier, all this work was going on before the serpent tempted Eve and the gardening got more difficult

(Gen. 3:17–19). Have you noticed that if we have no work, we have a tendency to invent it? Gardening and hobbies in our spare time, voluntary work of all sorts, carpentry, DIY, model-making. We were probably made to have a variety of working outlets and expressions, just like Adam. Clearly, God made us to enjoy work, find fulfilment and have a reason for getting out of bed in the morning.

I remember visiting a group of Canadian Indians in Shamattawa. Much of their society had collapsed, because they had been given houses to live in and welfare to spend but had no work to do. Yet the society had functioned perfectly well while there was a need to catch fish, hunt, make clothes and teach the younger generation to survive. I have seen exactly the same in Aboriginal homelands where the dignity of work has been replaced by welfare – leading to a generation of disillusioned young people who take to alcohol or petrol sniffing. I remember watching a young teenager walking around Ernabella, Australia, with a tin can full of petrol tied round his head – walking around all day with literally nothing better to do. Months later he was dead. The reason is not complicated: like every other human being, he was created to work, and when that work opportunity was removed he had nothing to live for.

The reformers and work

Almost without exception, the Reformers rejected the view that the *vita contemplatio* was the more truly Christian life. They taught that work, as well as leisure and contemplation, was a good gift of God. William Tyndale stated that there was no work better than another to please God, and was condemned for saying so. I remember this concept rather well, as it was impressed on me by Corrie

Ten Boom. As a young man I was working with YWAM and had been assigned the washing-up duties. I was silently doing the job, but in my heart I was wrestling with God. I was saying to him 'Look, I am cut out for preaching and spiritual work, this is a waste of time. I would be better off preparing for some new message.' I had said nothing out loud, so imagine my surprise when Corrie put her head round the door, pointed her finger at me and said 'Young man, I would far rather be doing what you are doing than what I am doing.' She walked off. I had never met her before, never once got to speak to her, and never saw her again. Her words, however, like Tyndale's, changed my theology.

Luther taught that God, in his providence, had placed each person in their place to do the work of that place. He said 'Just look at your tools, at your needle and thimble, at your beer barrel, your goods, your scales, your yardstick, your measure. You have as many preachers as you have transactions, goods and tools and other equipment in your house or home.'

Calvin was probably the strongest in his approach. It was Calvin's strength of view that shaped the application of the parable of the talents. He directly related the talents to everyday work and calling – in particular, trading. He stressed the practical application-orientated nature of these gifts. In the process he shaped the modern meaning of the words 'talent' and 'talented'. Like many after him, Calvin believed that each person is called by God to a particular type of work which, in its outworking, complements the work of others.

Paul's world of work

In the book of Acts we can see that at least six of the early apostles worked. They drew no fictitious line between spiritual and secular work. Paul uses the same phrases to describe his manual labour and his apostolic work. It is sometimes difficult to know to which he was referring. See how his words resonate with us in our experience of work; even in the toughest job of all. He tells slaves to work as slaves of Christ, which is exactly how he describes his own work for the Lord. He knocks the Christian caste system on the head by stating that 'there is neither . . . slave nor free . . . for you are all one in Christ Jesus' (Gal. 3:28 NKJV).

In 1 Thessalonians 4:11–12 he says 'Aspire to lead a quiet life, to mind your own business, and to work with your own hands, as we commanded you, that you may walk properly toward those who are outside, and that you may lack nothing' (NKJV).

And again in Colossians 3:22–4:2: 'Bondservants, obey in all things your masters according to the flesh, not with eyeservice, as men-pleasers, but in sincerity of heart, fearing God. And whatever you do, do it heartily, as to the Lord and not to men, knowing that from the Lord you will receive the reward of the inheritance; for you serve the Lord Christ. But he who does wrong will be repaid for what he has done, and there is no partiality. Masters, give your bondservants what is just and fair, knowing that you also have a Master in heaven. Continue earnestly in prayer, being vigilant in it with thanksgiving' (NKJV).

Work and me

My friend Niall Barry said to me one day 'You know you have his permission to be successful; you have his blessing to be successful.' I was, and am, so grateful for those words, but what an indictment that they should ever be necessary. I have met thousands of men and women who somehow feel less than spiritual, even guilty, because they are working day after day in a non-church environment. I have met many who can't really enjoy it because of various beliefs and pressures. I have met others who are so restless, so dissatisfied, so frustrated because they can't see a way out of the 'prison' of work. I want the words of my friend to be words of comfort and challenge to you. Wherever you are, as you read this, reach out and sense God's pleasure, his appointing and his anointing. Could you dare to believe that when you go to work, you are fulfilling a destiny written into the software of your life from heaven's programming department? Could you dare to believe that this is what you were created for? If you could believe that, what difference would it make? Destiny! Just about every Christian you speak to is looking for the thing that God has apprehended them for. Suppose this is it. Yes, you and your job, with your customer, your machines, your patients, your home. Work is not the antithesis of human fulfilment. We are not simply fallen creatures trapped in the curse of work. As new creatures in Christ we are called to express our restored image of God in the work we do and to the people we work with.

Ecclesiastes 3:22 says 'a man should rejoice in his own works' (NKJV). I work because it is good for me. God has given me work to enjoy. When I work there is something of the self-fulfilling joy of God that courses through my life. It gives meaning, it gives pleasure and it gives a wholesome outlet to express what God himself has placed within me. God himself works, and so when I work I touch, in some mysterious way, the Trinity itself. Like God, I should be able to look at what I do and say 'It is good.' I should be able to look at what I have achieved and be pleased with it. Work should also release personal fulfilment. Personal fulfilment is not the goal, but it is an outcome.

Where are your wings?

Even though the Reformers started well, the trouble was that the doctrine or understanding of the church was left basically unchanged from previous eras – dominated, in the main, by Roman Catholic teaching. The local church was still something separated from the real everyday lives of most of the saints out there. Inside, the ministers still taught from their pulpits and the church gathered was deemed to be primary. The rest of what the saints did was, by implication and definition, secondary. It followed that, over time, what had started well with Luther and Calvin did not end well. Today we are still faced with the divide between church and life: a divide that conquers the saints and keeps them tied to the sanctuary – the birdcage. And speaking of birdcages, where are your wings?

Our family was walking around Birdworld in the United States. We passed one area where, huddled and shrinking away in the darkness of some conifer bushes, there was a majestic golden eagle. The children were dismayed. Here was the most magnificent of all birds, held captive in a dark corner of the world by a small chain attached to a log. One of the boys wanted to jump into the enclosure and set the thing free, and had to be restrained.

All over the Christian world there are chained eagles. Logs of false teaching, chains of false expectation and false doctrine are holding down some magnificent men and women who, deep down, are longing to fly. They are longing for permission, for understanding, for conviction; longing to feel the wind of the Spirit blow under outstretched wings as they get lifted into the thermals high up in God's purpose. The time is here; the place is now. As you read, will you let the Word of God break those chains?

Will you let his Spirit breathe into your faint hope, your faint faith, and let him stir and lift you up to something higher?

It is good to ask the question: does my work use my potential as a human being? Does it encourage development or does it restrict me? The Pope has said that 'work is for people, not people for work. It is for our good and to develop us. We are not here to do it just because it has to be done.' A Gallup survey of over 20,000 people assessed the twelve key ingredients that make employees successful and likely to stay in their job. One of the twelve is 'the opportunity to do what I am best at every day'. In other words, does this job fulfil my human potential?

Work and human needs

The humanist Maslow outlined what he identified as a basic hierarchy of human needs:

- Physiological needs, such as a livelihood.
- Safety needs, such as a steady income, good safety procedures.
- Belonging needs, such as the need to associate with others, the sense of being together in unity. (In the past this could be met by trade unions. Current and increasing hire and fire methods are destroying values of loyalty and belonging.)
- Self-esteem needs, through exercising responsibility and initiative.
- Self-fulfilment needs – the realisation or actualisation of my potential, for example in creativity.

The biggest omission from all this is worship. One Hebrew word is used for both worship and work in

Scripture. Paul, picking up this theme in the context of us all being slaves of Christ, says 'Therefore, I urge you, brothers, in view of God's mercy, to offer your bodies as living sacrifices, holy and pleasing to God – this is your spiritual [or reasonable] act of worship' (Rom. 12:1). What do you think could be worship in your work? Let me offer some starting points:

- Offering my work to God – doing it for him.
- Seeing God in everything.
- Seeing what God is achieving through my work.
- Involving God in all I do.

We do God's will by working alongside God in bringing people and the earth to the place where they reflect the divine glory. We are co-workers, apprenticed to God.

Work is not everything

If we look for our ultimate self-worth or our primary significance in our work, we are in for a big disappointment. God designed us in such a way that our true and lasting significance can only be found in him – the creator of our work. He is there, in and through all that you do; he is waiting and wanting to be found by you, to fellowship with you and draw out all that he has created you to be. Search for him, he is there – in every opportunity, in every resource, in every person (even the problem ones). Of course, God is not the opportunity, the resource or the person – he is God. The Scriptures say, however, that God is in, through and over all things of the creation (Eph. 4:6), so don't be scared – go and find him and gather all the treasures he has placed in life into your heart and into your worship of him.

A good example of this was demonstrated in the film *The Towering Inferno*, in which a group of wealthy and successful people (the ones with significance in society) are put in a position where their significance counts for nothing. They are seen for what they really are when someone they considered a 'nobody' takes control and leads them to safety.

It is possible for work to replace God and become an end in itself, rather than being an expression of my love for him in it. Self-worth gets a lot of publicity these days and it is quite possible that work can become an altar on which I sacrifice much, if not everything, to the god of self-worth. It's a fine line and sometimes only the Spirit of God and his Word can divide between one and the other. It's a good question to ask him and our close trusted friends from time to time.

Work and leisure

We used to ask 'How many times have you heard a message on work as a high calling?' Today's question might add 'Have you ever heard a message on leisure?' One New England Puritan, Cotton Mather, used to preach a sermon on how to use leisure in the winter months. I wish I could get the transcript. Some Christians feel guilty about work, some feel guilty about their leisure and some feel guilty about both.

God made the world for us to rule over and care for. He made the elements for us to harmonise with. Ask me what my most spiritual times are and I won't take you to meetings, although I have been to some great ones. I will take you to the mountains and hills; I will certainly take you to my boat and the wind-kissed sea. When I sail, I could not be closer to God and his wonderful, wonderful world.

Jesus could take stress, but he also knew how to relax. On his own with close associates he would walk, eat, pray and sail on boats that he may well have made. Israel's life was ordained as a rhythm of work and rest. Each seventh day, each seventh year, and each seventh-times-seven year was a Sabbath for people, for animals and for the land itself.

One Anglican minister I know has tried this in his parish, particularly with his working parishioners in mind. If you have a function in the congregation, you are only allowed to exercise one, never more: house-group leader – nothing else; worship leader – nothing else. This is because the minister is determined not to make the gathering the centre. He divides the year into seven periods of seven weeks, which immediately gives three weeks that are holidays from meetings for all. Each set of seven weeks has one week off from gatherings. Once a month, the house-group leaders meet with the minister and team, and church-paid staff run the house-groups on those evenings. That way there is only one midweek meeting for everybody. It gives time for families, for work, for leisure and for outreach.

For many of us in today's brave new economy, work is less continuous and more task-oriented. Finding a rhythm of work and rest becomes more difficult. I find it almost impossible in my consultancy/training role. So for me, it tends to be seasons of refreshment and seasons of work in chunks of time. But I am so aware of the need to see work and leisure as partners in God's way of life in creation.

Work and outreach

I read or heard somewhere that Spurgeon looked out on a large Sunday congregation and commented that while he thanked God for the opportunity he was given to preach evangelistically in a church building, he believed this privilege to be extra-biblical. For Spurgeon, the task of evangelism belonged outside, not inside, the church. Archbishop William Temple echoed the same sentiment when he wrote: 'England will never be converted until the laity use the opportunities daily offered by them – various professions, crafts and occupations' (*Towards the Conversion of England*).

In recent years we have seen much emphasis on neighbourhood evangelism. But when Jesus wanted to define who my neighbour was, in the story of the Good Samaritan, he defined him as a travelling salesman in between hotel visits. For some, the neighbourhood will be the place, but for most this will not be the case. The place where we work is where we express his image and where we carry a tangible presence of God. I believe that it will be in the world of work that we will see the next great harvest. Let me share a story from a police HQ in Exeter.

In the summer of 1998, Sergeant Norman Amey was working in the Internal Affairs Department of the Devon and Cornwall Constabulary, at the police headquarters in Middlemoor, Exeter. He felt a burden for those around him who had not experienced the love of God and his fulfilment in their lives. Norman had been a Christian for many years, and was familiar with the concept of the Alpha course. He felt that Alpha could be brought into the workplace, and prayed that if this were the will of God, he would make it possible.

Dave Lazenby, a civilian employee of the police, commented to Norman one day that it would be good to run an Alpha course at HQ. Norman chatted with Roger Bartlett, a long-standing friend who was working at that time in the chief constable's office at HQ. Roger was excited by the prospect of running Alpha and a meeting was arranged where they called together all the Christians they knew of who worked for the police in the area. Norman takes up the story:

> We made no differentiation between police and support staff or between denominations. Anyone who found the teaching of Alpha acceptable was welcome. About eight people met together. There were representatives from most streams, including Baptist, Congregational, Assemblies of God, Church of England, Roman Catholic and Free Church. We have always been open to any background and I believe this is one of the strengths of the group, a witness to our colleagues and one of the precursors of blessings.
>
> Roger submitted a report to the chief constable, asking his permission to run an Alpha course in the headquarters complex. On 16 September 1998 Ian Main, a detective inspector in the force, tragically collapsed and died while playing squash at police HQ. He left a wife, Julie, and two daughters. Ian and Julie were both committed Christians. Ian was highly respected in the force. He was calm, likeable and solid. Although strong in his faith, he did not force it onto others, and many may not have known of his commitment to Christ. Before joining the force, he had been a professional footballer with Exeter City and Torquay United.
>
> Ian's death shook many of our colleagues. The funeral was held at Exeter Cathedral and the place was packed. Russell Fenn, leader of the City Community Church in Exeter, gave the address at the funeral. Russell was struck by the impact that Ian's death had on so many people and he wrote a letter to the chief constable at about the same time as Roger's report went in.
>
> The chief constable gave his permission for the Alpha course to run at Middlemoor, and the first 'Introductory Night' was held on 12 January 1999. There were about forty people at the opening evening, including

Christian 'supporters', and about eighteen completed the course. To date we have run a total of four courses and seen about thirty-five people complete it. This whole process has developed to the point where in May 2003 we brought together nearly one hundred police officers to work through the issues of God's destiny in our policing. The fruit we have seen from this includes the following:

- About five people have made first-time commitments.
- Several who had become disillusioned in their faith have been encouraged.
- Many have heard the truth laid out logically and fully for the first time.
- All those who completed the course were glad to have done so and many are still in touch. I believe that the seed has been sown for the future.
- There is a different spirit about the place, and Christians are no longer wary of speaking about their faith.
- The Christians have really been encouraged. They are able to talk and pray together. It is a real morale boost to see people around who are on the same side as you! It is not unusual to be chatting to another Christian and close the office door so that we can pray over the issues.

One of the people who came on the first Alpha course was the head of Occupational Health. He had been involved in the 'high church' in Scotland as a youth, but had had little involvement with the Christian faith since. His wife came on the third course. She made a commitment to Christ and many tears were shed in repentance. We prayed for her to receive the Holy Spirit. There was no outward sign of change, but we believed that God had worked. The following week, the whole group stood praying in turn, with hands laid on one of the leaders. As this new Christian started to pray, she burst into tongues and the whole group was touched. She subsequently had a prophetic picture, which greatly touched the same leader and opened up her life to the power of God.

Good works at work

Let me ask some questions as you read this chapter. I want to take you to five well-known scriptures:

- Habakkuk 2:14: 'For the earth will be filled with the knowledge of the glory of the Lord.' How many believe that? How will that be done? Will it be done through church meetings? There is only one way that it can be done and that is through working men and women.
- Ephesians 1:23: 'The church, which is his body, the fullness of him who fills all in all' (NKJV). How will his body fill 'all in all'? Is it possible to fill 'all in all' in church gatherings? Of course not. How are we going to fill all in all? In the place of work. Wherever that may be – paid or unpaid, servant or free, individuals in the home, young people in school, college or university, in our market, our factory, our office, our hospital, our court room.
- If the fivefold ministries of Ephesians 4:11–12 are to equip the saints for works of service, where will those works of service be? They will be where we are at work. Why is it, then, that probably 95 per cent of the ministry gifts operate in the congregation or its equivalent?
- If Ephesians 2:10 is right and God has good works that he prepared in advance for us to do, where will those good works be done? There is only one place – and that is when and where you work.
- In Matthew 5:16 Jesus says 'Let your light shine before men in such a way that they may see your good works, and glorify your Father who is in heaven' (NASB).

Where will those good works be? It has to be where we work.

I want to suggest to you that as we do these good deeds and good works, at that moment and in that place the Kingdom has come.

I want us to see clearly today that those good works, those good deeds, those works of service, filling 'all in all', God's glory covering the earth, cannot possibly be in church meetings. They can only be possible and take shape in one place, and that, ladies and gentlemen, is in the place of our everyday activities and works. Wherever God has placed us on his earth, his plan and his will for us is to fill that place with his presence and glory. And in that place God has works of service and good works already prepared for us to do. As faith begins to rise in us, as our eyes open to the longing in God's heart to put value in our workplace, to put significance for every one of us in the workplace, we may just begin to see our work as God sees it. He has created it for us from the beginning and it is the most spiritual activity we can engage in, if it's done for him, with him and through him. Work is wonderful, godly and eternal.

These good works can crop up in the strangest of places and in the strangest of environments. Hear how one person, who is a sign language interpreter, did this in the most harrowing of circumstances.

A psychotic had been released into the community, but was on controlling drugs. A well-meaning but sadly mistaken lady encouraged him to come off his medication. He subsequently brutally murdered her and beat her next-door neighbour to pulp. The murderer – now the accused – was imprisoned in a local police cell.

When my friend, let's call her Ruth, arrived, she found the accused kneeling in the cell, his bent frame taller than her full standing height! He was muttering rubbish and appeared threatening, so Ruth and the attending solicitor left.

Because of his violent strength, twenty-three policemen were involved in manhandling the accused, carrying him, with his arms and legs behind him, to a padded cell. In that place, a restraining hand covered every part of his body except his eyes. The accused – who was deaf and without speech – was terrified. What could Ruth do? She was angry at the way the accused was being handled, and out of her depth in the nature of the situation.

Somewhere in her spirit the reality began to dawn that this could be one of the works ordained for her, one of the good deeds God had prepared her for. She called out to God and began to stroke the accused's cheek. Signing to him to calm down, she told him that she was praying for him. Because speech was impossible, she asked him to blink twice if he could understand her signing, and each time he did so. Somewhere in the process, God's light penetrated the situation and, with nothing more than her signing language and the presence of the Holy Spirit and his angels, Ruth was able to see this violent, deranged murderer brought into a state where he was calm enough for normal procedures.

Angels at work

If work really is spiritual, and it is, then it should be no surprise that we find, as Daniel did, that angels turn up at work. If I asked you which stories in the Bible made you think of angels, you would probably give me Daniel and point to Matthew's early chapters. You know what I'm going to say, don't you? You're right – in both cases, angels manifested themselves into the lives of working men and women.

I am confident of angelic presence in my work. I know it is there every bit as much as in congregational settings, and probably more so – and I love it in both. It has been prophesied over me by a trusted person (who had no idea what I did), that as I spoke in the working world, angelic beings would be there alongside me.

Much of spiritual warfare to date has caused us to think that somehow the angels determine our spiritual reality. With a Hebrew, rather than Greek or Gnostic, understanding of the spiritual realm we can begin to think more clearly about the role of angels. In effect, it is humankind that determines spiritual reality, not angels. Angels were created by God to back up, garrison, intensify and surround the work that humanity does. Evil angels do this for evil work and righteous angels do this for good work. As Hebrews 1:14 (speaking of righteous angels) says, 'Are they not all ministering spirits, sent out to render service for the sake of those who will inherit salvation?' (NASB). So it is that when we do any good work, when we engage with creation and draw out from others and from our work the qualities, nature and strength of God, righteous angels gather around that work and help establish it. We have to stand there first – 'and after you have done everything, to stand. Stand firm then . . .' (Eph. 6:13–14).

Think about these verses. Consider also the many verses we looked at that spoke of the power and place of our good works. In particular call to mind Jesus' command to 'let your light shine' in and through all the work you do. As we do the good work, drawing out the divine nature in the settings we encounter, light begins to shine from the attributes, nature and power of God, for us, in, through and over all things in creation. This is why Jesus said that when people see our good works, the light from these works will shine to such an extent that people will be able to see our Father in the heavens above the earth. The righteous angels of God are those who ensure that the reality of our works is established in the heavens above the earth, that is, in the atmosphere through and over our families, our workplace, our communities and, ultimately, our cities and nations. As we 'good work' the creation, evil angels of darkness that have come in because of the evil works of man are displaced, and the angels of light, the flames of fire, light up the heavens overhead.

In Psalm 104, we find the corresponding passage to Hebrews chapter 1, regarding angels. As in Hebrews, it talks about angels as wind and fire. Where else do you hear that language? Wherever the Holy Spirit moves – and we know from practical experience and our reading of Scripture that the Spirit is at work constantly – we can expect angelic wind and fire. But the most remarkable fact in this passage is that angels are present and active in the practical world of work and works. Hebrews 12 reminds us that we have come to 'thousands upon thousands of angels'. There are enough for the working world, believe me. Chapter 13 reminds us not to forget to entertain strangers, for by doing so we may just entertain angels unaware. More, Lord, please!

And the angel called me sir

Enjoy this testimony from Tonni Wei, who was previously the Principal Director of Music of the Singapore Armed Forces:

> In 1986 the Singapore Armed Forces decided to get tough on the annual IPPT (Individual Physical Proficiency Test). If we failed our IPPT in the first year, a letter of warning would be

issued. The second year we failed, we would receive another letter of warning. Finally, if we failed in the third year, we would be discharged from the Military.

I have been in the Singapore Armed Forces for many years and my IPPT has always been a major problem to pass. In fact, I never did pass a single one before 1986. Needless to say, I failed my test that year also, and was required to take a re-test.

About two hundred other officers in my camp also failed the test and we had to attend remedial training for at least four weekends before we were permitted to take the re-test. The PTI (Physical Training Instructors) undoubtedly had a good time putting us officers through the training.

The gruelling sessions would always end with a 2.4 km run. I was completely shattered by the time it came to my first one. About a quarter of the distance into my run, a young man dressed in white T-shirt, shorts and running shoes pulled up effortlessly beside me and said, 'Sir, don't close your eyes'. As we ran along, he would give me instructions on how to run. For example, he would tell me at various points in the run when to lift my knees or stretch out and change my stride.

The next weekend, I met this young man again in the middle of my 2.4 km run, and he was there with me during all the subsequent training sessions.

I had never met this young man before, but I did not give it much thought, thinking that he was just another Physical Training Instructor recruited to help out with the large number of officers like myself who had failed their IPPT. What I did not notice then was that he was not dressed in the regular Physical Training Instructor outfit, nor was he wearing an identification badge. I was so exhausted after each training session that it never occurred to me to ask who this man was. I merely thought 'How kind of him to take such pains to help me.'

Finally, the day came for the physical fitness re-test. After going through all the various tests, I had accumulated only 12 marks. I needed 15 marks to pass. The last test was the 2.4 km run. I had never passed a run before, and was quite certain that I would not be able to get the three marks needed to pass my test. In order to get the three marks, it meant running the route one minute and twenty seconds faster. A mere ten-second increase would have been a great feat for me. I have short legs and I am partially flat-footed. Running was an extremely difficult physical activity for me. I was rather discouraged at that point, but I felt the Lord telling me not to give up since I had come this far. So I went for it.

As I was running, I felt the young man's presence with me. This time, I could not see him, but I could recall so vividly, at every stage of the run, his instructions. I could almost hear his voice calling out instructions just as he had during each training session. Towards the end, I could see the finishing line. The last hundred metres were on an uphill incline and I gave it all I had and crossed the line. While I lay exhausted on the floor, trying to catch my breath, I looked up and saw the young man standing in the crowd around the finishing line. He smiled at me and gave me a thumbs-up signal.

That was when I began to wonder about the identity of this man. After about half an hour – the time I needed to recover from the tremendous physical exertion – I went to check up on my performance. I was overjoyed to find that I had passed and had achieved my three marks with *one second* to spare!

I was becoming more and more curious about the young man who had helped me. The camp commander in charge of the remedial training happened to be a friend of mine. I went to his office and asked him whether he had recruited any new Physical Training Instructors for the training sessions. To my surprise, he said 'No'. In fact, all the trainers were the regular ones known to me.

To this day, no one knows who this young man was. I have never seen him since. I can still recall very clearly what he looked like: his face, his long legs and his physique. The only conclusion I could draw was that he was an angel, sent by God to help me pass my IPPT. From that point onwards, I never failed the test again.

I am filled with wonder that the Lord would do so much for me – he would send an angel just to help me through something as inconsequential as my Individual Physical Proficiency Test. This is a glimpse of his abundant love for me. There is nothing too small, no detail too unimportant in my life, for the Almighty God.

As we have looked at the Hebrew worldview in relation to creation, church and our work, we are now ready to build on the framework and begin to put some weight on the foundations. How do we do that? The next chapter gets us started.

7

Being and Building Church in the New Landscape

James

The Hebrew vision enables us to see the church positioned in all of our life and work in creation. Once this 'church as fullness' comes into focus in our understanding, we are in a place where we can more decidedly be that church. The following chapters look at the way in which we, as fellow workers with Christ, might build the culture in which the church as fullness can strongly emerge. The principles we are going to look at arise from a number of years spent working with, and observing, the growing culture of church in the world of work. Here we don't want to give an impression of arrival, but rather endeavour to look into aspects of the new landscape that we and others have, in part, been exploring and discovering. These principles should not be taken as some kind of ten-point plan for successful new landscaping. Certain methods will, no doubt, arise from what follows. However, it is important to stress that our intent here is to simply set some coordinates in place for the new-landscape church. We do not want to appear to be quickly building a ten-lane, method-driven highway through the forest to facilitate your easy and quick (non) arrival.

The Bible says that without vision the people dwell carelessly. The vision we need is a vision of the Son of God standing right through the present creation. The vision we need is a vision of his desire to fill up and fill out the spheres of business, health, family, marriage, education, government, the arts and the media.

Before we enter into this creation-encompassing vista, it's good to have what might be called a 'border-check'. This is both for those who, as the language says, are 'in ministry' and for those who are 'in work'. That being said, it is those in ministry, ether local church-based or otherwise, who are more in view here. The principles apply, however, to every person with a leadership gift or propensity. The reason why I need to cover this base – and, perhaps, in the eyes of some, over-emphasise the matter – relates to the dangers associated with lots of 'ministries' and local church leaders entering into what is called in some quarters 'market-place ministry'. If these bring with them ways of leadership, thinking and structure that have been the cause of many problems in the church as construct, they will muddy the waters for many others. Let us all tread carefully, tenderly – even slowly.

You can't create what already exists

The first thing we need to realise is that the church as fullness already exists in the landscape: it is already functioning. The problem has been that our doctrine or understanding of church has made it, for the most part, invisible to us. Hence the need for a theology of creation and of the church that enables us to see it. I make this point here because, too often, we leaders surmise that nothing is happening and so resolve to go and make something happen. We realise the need for market-place ministry and then set out to make things happen by organising this initiative and that, commissioning this group and that person to do works that will produce the results we envisage. Before we know it, our particular ministry, our new landscape 'institute', has taken to itself the mandate, as did the old (and still present) way of church leadership, and with that, moves to take charge of the people, the process and the centre yet again. If we realised that things were already happening, we would, hopefully, set out to work with what was, rather than build our own 'ministry' thing.

Many leaders find it strange when they read about cases in other nations where leaders of whole movements are scattered or killed and yet, within a few years, the church in that place sees incredible growth. As leaders, we must become aware that we are not in charge of the church as fullness. It has no king except Jesus and needs no king except Jesus. It does need servants, but it does not need managers pretending to be servants.

A number of ministries came together and decided to work out God's plan for their nation. They spent several days together and came up with a document that contained what they said was the 'strategy'. The difficulty was that a number of individuals and other ministries were not present when the plan was formulated. So, as you might imagine, when they heard about what had happened they were somewhat miffed. Then, to add insult to miff, they were 'encouraged' to submit their own agenda to the larger vision, to see where it fitted in to what was now 'God's plan for the nation'. It is natural for a person to think that what they are doing is central to them, but it is dysfunctional to think that it is central to everybody else. Too often, ministries looking for a following and in need of funding grasp a mandate and use it to grasp the centre, (humbly) thinking they are doing God and everybody else a favour.

History, as well as present observation, has shown that such a 'centre' usually ends up, over time, becoming just another sub-culture – separate from the mainstream culture and kept busy maintaining its own organisational and vested interests. Or worse, an organisation takes charge of a facet (or of the whole) of a culture/society. It is in this way that good ideas are gradually replaced by the 'rule of good ideas'. By trying to impose their vision of what that culture should look like, these centres can become instruments that diminish or even destroy the very culture they set out to bring into being (totalitarianism, market-driven corporatism and certain church hierarchies are in view here). We need, as leaders seeking to minister to the body, to expend less energy trying to create the new culture via our ministry and its supposed mandate, and more time working out ways to minimise our own drift/tendency towards the emergence of the old 'central tower of Babel' on the plains of the new landscape.

This needs to be stressed at the outset, because so much of our patterning in the old has to do with ministries leading the way and people following them. Any ministry or movement will grow in line with the DNA laid down in the first cells of its life. As we shall see, the more the new culture develops, the more we as ministers and elders will be called forth to serve with our gifts. There is a place for us in the church as fullness, but it's a different place to the one we have known. Let's surrender our need to be in charge at the border crossing, and enter the new landscape as a servant, a friend, an observer and a learner.

Works are not culture and culture is not work

A very important distinction needs to be made in the new landscape culture of church. It is a distinction between the culture and the works. The works we do take place in the context or setting of our particular culture. Hence, they are closely related but different. What it takes to build a culture is different from what it takes to accomplish particular works. Even though this is quite a simple distinction, we often confuse the two in our present way of doing church. Church leaders have, for the most part, taken oversight and management over both the Kingdom culture of the saints and the works of ministry that they do in and from the local church base. This results in too much authority being held by church leaders over the lives of Christians. Such an arrangement profoundly limits the scope and diversity of the culture in which the works of ministry are meant to be done.

In the church as fullness the saints are responsible for their own works of ministry in creation. The role of ministry gifts (these being the apostles, prophets, evangelists, pastors and teachers referred to in Ephesians 4:11) is to equip the saints. On the other hand, the role of elders is to assist in the development of a strong city-embracing Kingdom culture in which the saints and their works can flourish. One can, of course, be an elder and a ministry gift, but to collapse the roles into one office and use it to take charge of the culture and works of the saints is, to say the least, problematic. We need to have both a re-envisioning of the church and also what might be termed a 'separation of powers' if we are to see change come to this 'collapsed' church arrangement. Once Christ's body, the church, is positioned in all of creation and the distinction is made between the roles of the ministry gifts, the elders and the saints' works of ministry, much of our present confusion and the dysfunction it brings can, I believe, be resolved.

We will speak of this in more detail when we cover the subject of 'order' in the new landscape culture. Suffice it to say here that, as distinct from the old way of church, leaders in the new manage neither the works nor the culture of the saints: they are, as they should always have been, the servants of both. In this divine arrangement, their authority does not diminish: rather, it is finally realised for what God intended it should be. As elders and ministry gifts, whether from local church or business settings, let us concentrate on building a culture in which the good works of the saints can come to the fore. It is this work that will bear the fruit and shine the light Jesus intended.

A quote in relation to a pope

A biographer of Pope John Paul II, speaking regarding Poland and the overthrow of totalitarian rule, said of him that he came to the conclusion that political hegemony could only be countered not by oppositional politics but by cultural dissidence. A culture carries its own understanding of what it means to be human and it implicitly challenges opposing philosophies. Theatre, journalism, debate, an underground university – cultural institutions like these can send out dangerous messages about human rights, whatever words they employ. Seen from this point of view, the starter motor of historical change is not politics or economics but culture.

I leave to one side questions concerning John Paul's ecclesiology and ask that you take note of the wisdom expressed here. Culture is more powerful than power, and so we need to stimulate and resource the right culture rather than build a power base. As leaders, we must keep dispersing resources and no longer be kept busy accumulating and managing them.

But what about my church?

The above leads on to the question: what of the church as construct, the local or cell church? Where does it function at this time and how does it fit into the new landscape? In answer to this, I am sorry to inform you that I have to mention yet another book. It seems that among the many weaknesses writers have is the tendency to talk about other things they have written. I confess to such a weakness and now call on you to hear that confession. The book is called *Renegotiating the Church Contract* (Paternoster, UK, 2001). In that book I looked in some detail at the death now working its way through our present way of church. I wrote of a two-part process that is evident at this time of transition. One is the death process at work in our lives in relation to the church as construct. The other is the life process working to see the church as fullness emerge. These two are not separate: rather, they are two parts of the same equation for change. As an old way of church goes into death, the life of the new will be accelerated by the supply of ministry gifts, elders, the sacraments, the permission to gather and use the name 'church', all coming its way because of their release from the church as construct.

I mention this because we do not have the space here to repeat what is stated in *Renegotiating the Church Contract* regarding the journey into death by the church as construct. In the following chapters, we will be concentrating on the developing new landscape culture of church. As we do, it is important that we see the relationship between what is happening there and what is happening inside the church as construct. The two are strongly related and we need to understand that relatedness if we are to see the Platonic stronghold – the divided thinking that set up the church as construct in the first place – overthrown in our thinking and rendered unable to dominate the emerging church as fullness. The old form has to die a death: it cannot dress up in suit and tie and move its business into the church as fullness. So, on a more positive note, let's now turn to see what it might take to resource, serve and build the culture in which the already existing church as fullness might thrive.

New landscape observations

There are seven words that, to my mind, speak of the culture-building process now under way: Agreement, Language, Parables, Resource, Pioneers, Gathering and Order. Over the past few years I have worked to transition a local congregation away from its orientation around leadership at the centre. I have also been active as a ministry gift in health and business networks to nourish a culture in which the 'church as fullness' is emerging. I cannot give you any South American set of calculations in relation to my success. I believe, however, that I can offer some good principles and observations that I have seen in action during that time. In line with what I have said about the dangers of ministries or persons setting up central shop in the new landscape plane, I have sought to merge into, rather than be a leader of, a culture. That is, I have not tried to push or pull, but rather to relate and come alongside, to salt and leaven a little and then sit back and observe. I say this to guard against the tendency for anyone to think that the seven words I have mentioned above were my plan, my vision or my goal for what I set out to do. It was only after several years that I felt I needed to summarise for myself what I had seen: in particular, to note what kinds of things were called forth during the different phases of growth I had witnessed.

Once I had settled on an outline of what I had observed, that is, once I had written down these seven words and was content that they were an adequate description of what I had experienced, I was able to look at them from different perspectives. To my mind, what is suggested by these words is a way of both recognising and building the culture in which the church as fullness can arise. This is not to suggest that they be applied in some kind of rigid or dogmatic way. This, of course, is the danger in presenting such a list, particularly to those whose gift is pragmatism. 'Right, now, let's do the permission thing. Next, we need some resources. OK, you over there; get me a parable.' These words can, of course, suggest different actions that might be taken, but they are, first and foremost, given to assist our vision of the already emerging culture of the new church. They should not be taken as a strictly chronological progression.

While resources were being developed and supplied, people were already gathering in the place of their work, agreeing with each other to be the church in that place. What these words speak of relates more to the particular need or hunger I saw more strongly expressed by those in the culture during different phases of their growth. So, in summary here, the development that these words suggest is, to my mind, progressive, but the situation they describe is very fluid and they can also interact and happen together. Finally, these seven words are simply coordinates on a paper map and, as such, are some distance from the complexity of the real and muddy land itself. It is important that we do not take these as being 'the vision' – they are not the vision, they are an observation. So, with all those safety checks in place, let's begin to unpack them.

Roll on reversals

One of the first things I noticed about these seven words was the way in which they operated, almost in reverse of what current leadership wisdom would teach. We have been taught by leadership experts to get a vision and take charge (order); get a group of people to work with and under us (gathering); then, as leaders, begin to break ground so that the people can follow us (pioneer). As things grow, you bring in more 'resources' to meet the demands now placed on you. You will now be able to keep increasing the number of church-based ministries (parables) that express your vision and extend your reach. As you do this, you will set up an enduring church with a strong culture (language) and this will further facilitate and enable people who come in to minister in and from the base you have established (agreement). What this reversal creates is a culture that is kept inside a construct and under a leader. It makes for a culture of church that is dependent, rather than one that is interdependent and creation-encompassing. It is when we set the creation, rather than the congregation, as our starting point, that a reverse of the above process will lead us to a very different outcome.

The second thing that might be helpful to mention up front in regard to these seven words comes from my good friend Nigel Sykes. Nigel lectures on the MBA programme at Warwick University, England. He, in line with the apostle Paul's usage of the word, is a saint. Over many years God has, I believe, given to Nigel a way of seeing work that is more closely aligned to creation reality than any other I have seen. It draws on wisdom from other business approaches and models, using some of the elements found there, but adding much more to profoundly map the people, product and process cycles in a business.

Suffice it to say that his approach serves to create a work environment where gifting, innovation and transition can regularly happen, and where control, stagnation and rigidity do not (or at least they find it very hard to dominate because of the working environment the model helps set up). As I was showing Nigel what I had observed in relation to the emerging culture, he let out a gasp and said 'These seven words correlate to the different phases of the business model.'

As we talked over the similarities, I was struck by the extent to which they did indeed match up. A healthy culture establishes an environment that encourages healthy work to emerge. If we build together a culture that is of the Kingdom, the good works of the saints in every creation sphere will arise in and from that culture. Again, it's the culture that holds the key to the good works. The stronger the culture we build, the more potent the work that rises from it. Hence the need to take the time to build the right environment in which the church as fullness can rise.

When I speak of not heading out to do too many things up front, taking time to build culture and see what emerges, you may be thinking that I am suggesting a go-slow approach. You may be itching to get out there and make your impact, thinking that this will get the job done sooner, better, stronger. On the contrary, what I am suggesting will, I believe, be the greatest accelerator to the new. That sounds like a sales pitch, I know, but I declare this with such confidence because it lines up with the teaching of Jesus and Paul concerning the little seed and the small speck of leaven. When we build in line with the old, front-end, hierarchical leadership style, we find that initially things do happen more quickly. People respond more easily to things that are clear, simply and easily showcased inside a meeting, and done by others with resource and gifting. However, down the track in, say, five, ten or twenty years, these same people wake up to find that things inside the construct are slowing down. Inertia sets in as the machine now consumes more energy to keep itself going than it can get in each week. Too many movements down through history have simply collapsed under the weight of their own self-infested glory. As the saying goes, 'It's not how you start, it's how you finish that matters.'

If a butterfly flaps its wings in the office . . .

It should not amaze me, but it does, how much movement happens when the focus of the culture comes to bear on the good desire God has gifted into every heart. How wonderful it is to see one, then three, then nine, then forty and then, all of a sudden, innumerable people moved by that good desire to 'good-work' the earth towards the fullness. Things that are alive do not need lots of high-priced oil and maintenance to keep them on the road. Let us build the new in line with Jesus' strategy and see the largest of trees emerge – so much so that the birds of the heavens (in line with the creation mandate given to Adam) will be able to come and nest in its branches. Such a tree will offer great shelter to many. It will be able to endure the seasons of change and will bear its fruit year in and year out. It will be able to do this because of its grounding in the earth, the strength of its stature in Christ and its reach towards the heavens. It will take time for people who are accustomed to being led by something (and someone) else to trust their own good desire and their own discernment in taking Kingdom initiatives. Hence the need to establish a culture that draws them out into this way of life and work. We need to see established an environment in which the saints can be safe, encouraged and resourced to gather, through the work of their hands, the eternal inheritance into their hearts. Let's start by giving them permission.

8

If Two or More Agree

James

Culture is another word for the way people live and work together. For this reason, the starting point for building culture has much more to do with relationships than with teaching, resourcing or leadership. One of the most powerful elements of any relationship is trust that gives agreement. If the people we value and love trust us regarding the things we desire to do, we are able to experience so much more strength and agreement in relation to those works. If no one believes in what we are doing, it is very difficult for us to believe in it ourselves. If we do not sense or know agreement, things like anger, money or reputation might fuel our work for a time but will not enable us to create the kind of good work that brings in the fullness spoken of in Ephesians.

I remember reading a business magazine article in the waiting room of an accountant. It spoke of the number of company managers who had worked hard and done very well until they had succeeded. Within a year or so of this success their businesses failed. The writer spoke of how analysis showed that many of these people (men in particular made up the examples) had been driven by a desire to prove to their fathers that they could succeed. That is, they wanted their father's affirmation, but did not have it, and set out to make their fathers believe in them. So it followed that when they did succeed and the sense of affirmation was still not there, they lost the motivation that had fuelled their journey to the top. The power that comes from affirmation and agreement, and in particular that which comes from our Father God through mentors, friends, family and those in authority, is crucial. Whatever the culture we identify with, be it church or societal, those who are affirmed will live and thrive and those who are not affirmed will remain weak, become destructive or simply die.

That is why we read so much in the teachings of Christ regarding agreement. 'Again I say to you, that if two of you agree on earth about anything that they may ask, it shall be done for them by my Father who is in heaven. For where two or three have gathered together in my name, I am there in their midst,' said Jesus in Matthew 18:19–20. When there is an agreement between people on earth concerning each other; concerning the work before them; concerning the divine purpose to fill all things, then our Father in heaven above moves to establish and accomplish the good desire of heart expressed and agreed upon. Not only that, but also the Son of God is there in the midst to help those in relationship with him fill out and fill up the creation with the work they have together agreed to do.

The matter of agreement is stated quite clearly in the verse prior to the ones we have just read. Jesus says 'Truly I say to you, whatever you bind on earth shall have been bound in heaven; and whatever you loose on earth shall have been loosed in heaven' (verse 18). The word 'bind' means to forbid, and the word 'loose' means to permit. The imagery is drawn from a legal context: the sense of it is that whatever is not permitted in heaven should not be permitted on earth, and what is permitted in heaven should be permitted on earth. This truth, as one can see, flows naturally on to the teaching found in the verses that follow. God has said that he will 'fulfil every desire for goodness and the work of faith with power' (2 Thes. 1:11–12). However, for that desire to find its way into work, and for that work to be done with faith, people need to be given the power of agreement.

The reason why much of the work done by the body of Christ in the spheres of creation has little effect is that it is done with little or no agreement. Yes, church leaders do at times affirm work, but more often than not it is in terms of it being a place to fulfil one's responsibility, raise money for church initiatives and witness to the Gospel. Beyond that there is often little agreement, teaching and resourcing relating to the saints' work in creation. Right now, all of heaven is waiting for the church as fullness to arise in every sphere of life. That permission exists in heaven right now for us. The bill has been passed; the law is on the books above us. What remains is for us to give the saints the permission and release that will enable them to be and build the church as fullness. In some church settings this is now changing, but the kind of agreement necessary to see the body arise in creation is still a way off.

It is not just a matter of saying, as leaders, that we release people to their work, if almost all of the naming rights, resources and affirmation relating to being church remain inside our building. One leader said to me concerning a member of his congregation: 'We recognised that she had a ministry out there and so we released her to that.' My response to him was, 'What did you do after that?' He blinked, in answer to my question. He had released someone from having to minister primarily from the local church but, as a leader, did little or nothing to help her succeed. Failure to make eternal marks in time is not always the fault of the struggling saint. Failure often happens because there is little or no culture of affirmation, no right given to stand as the church in Jesus Christ in creation, no resource of ministry gift and no fathering by elders. If we are to break out of this cycle of failure we need to acknowledge that perhaps it is our ecclesiology and not the saints that is failing us.

Dangerous permission

When we, as leaders, extend the power of agreement to the saints in relation to being church in all of life and work, we need to understand that this may well mean that they will be released to such an extent that they may not come back to our particular congregation. If our release is conditional, then it is not release. There is a time for nurture and there is a time for release. We seem to be very good at the first and not so good at the second. An understanding of the church as fullness and the release and agreement given to people to be that church has many ramifications that we need to face as church leaders. It is best that we nurture, that we trust, and that we release the saints to their inheritance in creation.

I know that for some, alarm bells will be starting to sound here. One might at this stage express the following concerns: 'If we follow this to its conclusion, doesn't it mean that the housewives will disappear into their homes, the doctors into their surgeries, the business operators into their companies, and so on? One might well say: How can the body of Christ demonstrate unity if everyone has gone their own separate way? How can I, as a pastor, benefit from the insight of the business operator, the doctor or the voluntary worker, if they all go their separate ways? Isn't this robbing the body of Christ? Am I free to do exactly as I want? No. I am part of a body, with joints, relationships, responsibility, accountability and serving. If we only met in relation to one small part of our life, say, our employment setting, how horrific that would be!'

These are good questions, the kinds of questions and concerns we need to feel the weight of. For the moment, I will let them sit. It's a bit like Paul's teaching on sin and grace and the way it precipitated the question and implied assertion: 'Are we to continue in sin so that grace may increase?' (Rom. 6:1). Martyn Lloyd-Jones said, concerning this statement, that if the truth of what Paul was saying was actually comprehended, it should lead to such a response from those concerned that this teaching would lead to lawlessness and anarchy. We will seek to cover these bases of concern as we go along, but for now, I want to issue a further challenge to the status quo. The matter of the congregation leaving us, as pastors, and no longer attending all or some of the meetings we hold on their behalf is not, to my mind, the first issue that we need to face. It is the present status quo that makes it hard to re-envision the emerging shape of the gatherings in the church as fullness. Before we can reach a place where we will be able to do so, we need to reposition the pastor, moving him or her out, much further out, from their church centre, to serve and equip the saints for life and work in creation. It is from that new vantage point that the pastor will be better able to see the emerging diversity and new-found unity of the body of Christ. From that vista, we will all be better able to understand and appreciate the new ways in which that body might express its unity in gatherings that are particular to our sphere of work and those that encompass our family and/or local community.

When congregational leaders release the saints it is not necessarily the end of the relationship. We need to grow up further by continuing the journey with them into the work that they do. It is when we release them to their work as the church that we give them the choice to be in relationship with us. For too long, church life has been about loyalty to leaders, to their visions and rights over the people and the process. It's time we had more loyalty to the saints from those who are called to be their servants. The more freedom the saints are given to choose relationship with those in leadership, ministry gifts and elders, the stronger and healthier those relationships will be. We, as leaders, cannot hold on to the saints inside our church construct, calling them by that strange and unbiblical name 'my people', and pretend we are giving them the power of agreement they need to penetrate the darkness and shine the light into their world.

Where do I go to get agreement?

In many instances, it will be hard to gain the kind of permission you need from those in church leadership. This is because the doctrine of the church gathered as church central still prevails in most places. It is good to seek whatever level of agreement you can for your work from those who lead in your local or cell church. Tell them what you are doing, share your heart's desire and struggle, and tell them that you value their agreement. Let them know that you want to hear more from the Word of God in relation to the nature and purpose of your work. As you do, you will draw them out and give opportunity to them, as ministers, to grow and begin to encompass more of the new landscape.

Further to this, we need to seek agreement from peers and mentors in our work setting. In many ways (though I wouldn't want to exaggerate this) this is more important than the agreement you might gain from your minister. Remember, you are the church and you have the agreement of heaven to be and build that church in all of life and work. This is not a recipe for rebellion: rather, it is a word that informs you that God trusts you and has called you to function as the church where you live and work. We need the power of agreement from our colleagues and workmates and we need it right there in the place Christ has called us to be his body. We need agreement, and lots of it, to survive and thrive in our place of work. Heaven is ready and waiting to match the power of agreement that we establish in our work settings with nothing less than 'It shall be done' by my Father.

A friend was being offered a job to transform the culture of an organisation that is employed by larger corporations to transform their own cultures. He was considering the position and we met for coffee. He talked about it for a time and then, somewhat unsure of how to word it, he said to me 'I suppose what I am after is your agreement to do it, in a sense, your permission, and I want your help to do it.' I said yes on both counts, we shook hands in agreement, and then I asked him to help transform my own personal culture in the process.

It is, of course, best that those we enter into agreement with are Christians, but sadly, at times, we may find it very hard or impossible to locate them. In most settings, however, we will generally find people who may not be Christians but who love truth and want to see the good arise. We need also to develop a level of agreement with them. Obviously, this will not have the intensity or effect that an agreement between saints will have, but it is very important that we look out for such alliances. I am not speaking here about life-long covenants, but rather agreement to pursue and do what is good. Scripture records many instances where holy prophets would not touch unholy heathen, only to find that God was working all along to see these people come to truth. The building of a way of church that is interfaced from the start with those in the world is a critical difference between the old and the new expression of church. All too often we build a church sub-culture, working hard over many years to make it strong so that we can reach out from it. In time we find that we have grown a congregation very much removed from the surrounding culture; one that has very little capacity to salt, leaven and light the city. And why? Because it has become too much of a lump to penetrate the world.

Again, it may be difficult to find saints willing and wanting to agree. However, things are on the move and more and more Christians are taking permission to build with others the new culture of being church. So search them out. Pray that they might surface and, when they do, relate to them with a view to establishing the power of agreement between you. If you can't find any agreement, ring someone up and tell them to agree with you. When they do, write it on your wall, date it for future reference and keep creating!

What's there to agree on?

What are we in fact seeking permission to do? Fill the creation and grow up in Christ to the third heaven is a good starting point. This, however, might be a bit much to bite off in one sitting! That being said, it is important to know just what and where Jesus is in all of this. He is placed right there with you, in that finance industry, in that health sphere, in that company being downsized, and he is seeking to fill creation through the work you do and the relationships you engage in. Closer to heart, home and office, we are looking for agreement in relation to our struggles and heart desires. We are searching for strong permission to search out the attributes, nature and power of God in the sphere of work that we are engaged in. We are looking for fellowship where we can begin to share more deeply what it is to be the church and build the church in all of life and work.

Agreement is not simply a quick prayer or even a set of prayer meetings. Too often, agreement has been reduced to workplace prayer meetings that last for seven months and then fade away. Once you have prayed for the boss to be converted twenty times and for the warlock on the second floor handling the office supplies to move out of the premises and stop sending memos about you to the CEO, there is not much you can say. I don't want to downplay prayer here, but it is important to realise that powerful prayer arises from powerful relationships, and powerful relationships come from strong engagement with the work, in line with the divine purpose in that sphere of work. A friend of mine once did the rounds of city-based prayer meetings in London. He came back saying that most of them prayed and talked as if they were refugees stranded in a foreign country, surrounded by the enemy, hanging out for the Sunday rescue package to enable them to get through another week of exile. We need more than this if we are going to fill creation. Agreement is relationship with each other, with the work itself and with Christ who is in and through that work. Like most good things, it takes time, desire and commitment. Heaven is in agreement – let's now translate that to the earth beneath our business.

Chartered accountants rule

John is a chartered accountant. He came to see me as his pastor around eight years ago. At that time I was involved in pastoring a congregation and managing a medical and counselling centre we had set up from our local church base. John said to me 'Why are you spending most of your time here building up this team and managing this place when people like myself in finance and my wife in health need you to come and help us as well?' So I took his advice and responded by spending more time with both of them.

At that time John used to meet on a monthly basis with six or so other accountants. In their meetings they would open in prayer, discuss tax laws, technical issues and other such things that accountants do, and then close in prayer. It was good fellowship but, one might say, rather tame. Over time, as John and I shared concerning the emerging shape of the church and his good desire in relation to the world of work, John found stronger permission to be and build the church as fullness. Encouraged by this, he began to contribute more to the group, encouraging his colleagues to share more of their heart desire and to pray more directly for one another.

Shoot ahead eight years in time. John has now joined with six of these chartered accountants in an office complex that constitutes the largest accountancy practice in our area of the city. They have agreed to join as Christians in business together, to shine light, to be accountable to each other and, in effect, to be the church in all that they are and do in work. One of their number said recently 'This place is now holy ground to me, it's where I work for God and in God.' Another one said that this group was, for him, the most meaningful Christian fellowship he had experienced: 'I can say things here and I can pray things here that I can't pray or say on Sunday.' In the practice there are saints from Baptist, charismatic, Catholic and Pentecostal congregations and cultures, but they are all one church at work together. In their conference room at the centre of their office, they regularly pray for each other and for their clients, they work through issues and support one another.

Who would have thought it would be a group of accountants that God would use to break ground in this way, being the church at work and seeing their work as integral to being that church? I told a pastor who had a building three hundred metres from the office complex about what had happened in his territory. When I did, he looked rather stunned, and I could tell that what I was saying was messing with his doctrine of church. I then encouraged him, gave him permission to relate to, serve and resource them, in line with his own gifting and desire to build the body in his local community. I knew he wanted to, and in time he will, but there was some ground he had to cover in himself before he could fit what had happened into this worldview of church.

Here is a quote from John concerning their first day together in the office:

> We all signed the contracts that day and agreed to gather in our new premises at 5 p.m. on Friday 30 June 2000. To paint the picture, we were the proud tenants of a very impressive office that none of us could afford individually. After the Lord had taken care of some very extreme obstacles, we were sitting in the place God wanted us to be – strongly united.
>
> As we gathered in the boardroom of these premises, we all sat quietly, but we wanted to scream with joy. Someone yelled out a 'cooee' (Australian for loud noise) and we all joined in (as chartered accountants tend to do). We talked, agreeing together about the extent of God's providence in seeing seven Christian accountants and their practices coming together in this way. We did not know where this would take us, but we did know that God had a big plan. Quietly, we were all feeling God's presence and power in our gathering. We began to pray and the heavens opened and angels

responded. We truly felt the Lord's rejoicing in our meeting. Prophetic prayers began to rise and were declared loudly. Words of wisdom and knowledge were spoken. Angels were posted at the doorway. Tears were shed.

For over an hour the prayers went out and no one could move. Finally, we all took hold of each other's hands and a moving prayer of unity was prayed. The awe of the moment held us suspended in time and space. A beacon had been lit to call us to this place to commence reclaiming lost territory for the Lord. All of us were sealed, joined one to another and to the Lord himself. We were shown an arrow, true and straight, one ready to fire and one that we would be called to follow. We were truly on a journey of life in the place of our work with our beloved Lord.

The power of agreement can travel a long way if we allow it to.

9

New Landscape Language

James

I would imagine that we have all been in a situation where the language being spoken by everybody around us was one that we did not understand. I was at a dinner party with a cousin in France and her husband began to tell a joke. Knowing that my French is non-existent, he condescended to tell it in English. I was following the rather long story line that gradually got funnier as the situation described got more complex, and was, of course, looking forward to the punch line so that I could politely laugh in English. Then suddenly, for no reason except perhaps that the joke was coming to its climax, the fellow started speaking in a French/English mix. As he did, the other Parisians in the room began to tune in more strongly and became so animated that in response he jumped totally across to French. As the joke reached its now French climax, and everyone in the room broke into French laughter, I politely smiled and let out a foreign chuckle. Still, to this day, I sometimes wonder how the joke ended.

Without understanding of the language, it's very hard for us to know what's happening or to join with each other in a happening. If we are to see the new landscape culture of church emerge we need to have a way of expressing, describing and telling it to each other.

I am not speaking here about us developing another brand of jargon – of learning some obscure language to be spoken by an elite in candlelit rooms at the edge of civilization. Rather, I am speaking of the language of Scripture; of the language of Paul and Jesus; of phrases that speak of 'all creation under heaven' (Col. 1:23); of Christ filling the present created order; of our being and building the church that we are, and other such understandings that come more clearly to light under a Hebrew sky. This is not some mysterious language that comes from outside into our lives. Rather, it is a language that speaks of the way God has made things to be, of the way God has designed us as his people, his body, his church. It is intrinsic language. As such, it is more natural, more essential, more created than any other utterance on earth. Plato has given us a language of division. We need to replace that with the language of unity. Here again I am speaking of worldview, of seeing the Platonic worldview dispatched and the Hebrew vision that is taught in Scripture rise in our mind, surface in our workplace and live in our relationships.

Where language goes, we, with others, can go. If there is no language there is no expression, and if there is no expression there is no relationship, no agreement, no permission, no shared life. If the enemy can curtail our language and bind it in and under small and divided places, then he has bound and gagged us. As one person said, multiplied millions of saints are going to work each day and most of them haven't a clue about the relationship between their work and the purposes of God on earth. Remember those prayer groups in the city, the refugees hanging on for Sunday supplies? We need to transform these saints from the back foot to the front line. To do this we need to equip them with some night vision, give them a description of the land they have to occupy, supply them with some language they can use to gather intelligence and join forces to overcome.

At the present time, these saints cannot see each other as the church in the place of their work. This is because most of the sight lines and language paths come from and return to the church as meeting or 'construct'. This situation is portrayed in the following graphic:

Living as a saint in a divided universe is like being in a dense jungle. You can hear the sounds of people close to you and occasionally you run into one or two. However, because there are few or no tracks in that jungle, most people remain isolated, never really connecting. Many are lost in the mist, spending their lives wandering around in a haze. We need to create trails in the world of work, paths that enable people to travel, to meet, to carry goods and build settlements. As the saying goes, 'it's a jungle out there'. If we are to change that, we need first to change the language, and if we are to change the language, we need to change the worldview responsible for tangling our communication in knots in the first place.

The truths relating to the Hebrew vision of creation and the church as fullness have been covered in part in the earlier chapters of this book, and in more detail in *The Church Beyond the Congregation*, so we do not need to cover them again here. What does, however, need to be stressed is the importance of not laying these truths on too thick in the beginning phases of building the new landscape culture. Why not?

We have become addicted to teaching in our present culture of church. We hear so much of such intensity and import so often that much of the meaning in what we hear is lost before we drive out of the church car park. Because of our more Greek or rationalistic approach to truth, we think that the more we know, the more we can achieve – but this is not the case. If we know too much more than our life experience can match, that knowledge can begin to work against our maturation. So often, we arrive in our head but our life is still a long way off the mark. We have nodded in approval, we have responded at an altar call, and so we feel content, satisfied and ready for the next bit of information from the next sermon next Sunday. Our way of teaching is in dire need of examination. It is producing saints who know too much and have so little time to do anything with what they know. We have created sermon tasters, preacher consumers, church shoppers, and the immaturity this has entrenched now sets the church agenda for what must come next. We need to look again at the teaching strategy of Jesus, following the master teacher as we seek to build according to Kingdom specifications. How did Jesus work the divine curriculum?

The amazing understatement of God the Son

One of the most remarkable things about Jesus, to my mind, is how much he didn't tell people. I can take stock of things like the incarnation, virgin birth, miracles, resurrection and ascension; because God can do things like that. However, when the person who knows everything about the universe comes and tells us the things that Jesus told us, I am struck with wonder at his understatement. Don't get me wrong, I think what Jesus taught was profound, divine and stunning in its simplicity and strength. I am more struck, however, by the amount of space he left in his language; by the gaps in his parables; by the many hidden things he left unexpressed in the things he did express; by his words that sent out an invitation to enquiry; by the questions he left lingering, like the memory of taste on the tongue; by the way he took understanding away from the wise and gave it to the unlearned in a way that confused and excited them. How different this is to the tell it all, explain it all, map it all, wrap it and sell it all production-line preaching we have fallen for in our consumer age.

Jesus left space in his teaching so that people could enter in and discover their heart desire; so that sons and daughters might discover the deep gifting in their soul; so that saints might take their own journey in real time into creation. He wanted the invitation he gave to draw the image bearers through the thorns of life and work, there to lay hold of the attributes, nature and power of God in, through and over all things.

The profundity of the Hebrew vision taught in Scripture is that it is a sketch, an outline, a perspective. Like compass points on a piece of paper, it suggests the way of the journey ahead. It points to things you'll need to know, tells you of things you'll need to have. It gives you a feel for the landscape so that when you get there you'll recognise its contours as familiar territory and, conversely, know if you are straying and need to turn back. As distinct from much of our method, moral, truth-as-concept kind of teaching and preaching, the Hebrew vision of the heavens and the earth cannot be put into practice by a congregation centred on a building. It cannot be showcased to inspire and direct the saints coming on a Sunday towards the local church's mission. As when gazing upon an incredible sunset, one enjoys the grandeur, the distance and closeness of colour, but can never fathom what is seen. Imagine what Adam felt when God pointed to a bird flying in the sky and then said to him 'Adam, will you rule over the birds of the heaven for me?' 'Sure, I can do that' would not, I think, have been Adam's first response. I picture a rather bemused but polite look coming over his face as he listened to God's plan for the birds.

Revelation progressively comes our way as we arrive at the place in ourselves and in creation where that revelation has been, shall we say, stored or hidden by God. It is as we grow up in all things that we journey from one level of glory to another. Each stop on our journey through the heavens contains its own special measure of the attributes, nature and power of God. Each person, place and thing is ready, when the relationship is right, the time is full and the agreement is reached, to release the inheritance it contains into our heart. Jesus was in no hurry to tell all before all was ready. He was in no hurry to reveal all before people got there. So then, let us not think that we can teach the new into existence. We must good-work it in, in relationship; out there in life, in agreement; together as one body, the church. That takes time, time in which we can share lots of good truths as long as we don't mistake what is taught or preached for what is real and has arrived. Preaching is at best a rehearsal for reality, but if we mistake it for the main act, bad reviews from men, angels and heaven will continue to come our way.

This is, I would hope, not a discouragement to teaching and preaching with passion. There is a need for that. I personally like speaking. I have had to train myself, however, to be quiet and let much more space invade the landscape. As you can see from all these words, I have not conquered my habit entirely, but have shifted across to writing. I'm taking my time getting over my word habit.

The approach I am suggesting is one in which we don't swamp the landscape with teaching tapes and videos and, in particular, that bane of Christian life – the method men. Dare I say it: we are obsessed with product, particularly product that has buttons and levers to push and pull, things to do and say and when to do and say them. I am aware that this book is a product, and so again cannot claim total immunity from prosecution. Jesus, I believe, was very clear in his attempt to both inform and confuse everyone, including his disciples. What is of particular note was that he hardly ever spoke of methods.

When he finally said something straightforward, such as 'I came from my Father in heaven and I am going back there', the response to such clarity of communication was such that one of the apostles said 'Lo, now you are speaking plainly and are not using a figure of speech. Now we know that you know all things . . . by this we believe that you came from God' (Jn. 16:29–30). What a strange response. Who would have imagined that a proof of the deity of Christ would be his capacity to speak normally like everybody else! It is very clear that Jesus did not set out to be very clear. The reason he gave for this was that it is only when you do his teaching that you come to know that it is of God (Jn. 7:17).

So, we don't need too much teaching up front. We need to weave truth and sight into the relational mix and allow a hunger for more truth to be the signal for more truth to be given. The less we give closure to people, the more they will have to learn to find their own arrival places in life. We need to understand that most of what we currently preach is not understood or acted on, and thus is not assimilated into people's lives. If you are a pastor, you have probably been in a situation where you have preached your heart out for years about a particular topic. Then someone from the congregation comes to you and says that God taught them this truth, the very truth that you have been teaching for years, and then adds insult to injury by telling you that you should preach on this. The major reason for this is that people only get what their life is ready to handle.

I am advocating that we work with this reality rather than against it. If we have a group of saints who meet in relation to the business or health sphere, for instance, don't think that anyone will get it simply because you said it. As you speak, the things that will make sense will be the things that are in their experience. As you teach, the things that will ignite interest will be the things that are in their desire. As you converse, the things that will challenge will be the things that are within their reach, just up ahead of their present experience. This is how God made people to be and to learn. He always intended that knowledge should be woven into life and not overtake it.

Knowing this, we can follow Paul's advice when he suggested that our speech always be with grace; seasoned, as it were, with salt. If we get too excited or are desperate for sermon fodder to get us through the next few months of our preaching schedule, then too much salt will end up in the soup. We may be getting excited at the interest being shown among those in our industry, think that it's time for a study course to be launched and begin to sign people up. This may well be the best thing to do: I cannot say. But I feel I should issue a warning – don't let learning get ahead of reality and relationship. For once you have said it all several times over and nothing much has happened, there's not much else you can say. Once we have finished a ten-week series on the Hebrew vision and the initial excitement has died down, we can, of course, start another sermon series on another topic. The problem with this is that the other topic has probably been done to death as well. Don't declare all that's in the heart of what is emerging: firstly, because you don't know it, and secondly, because even if you did you would be – as Proverbs indicates – a fool to do so.

It's the same as with a child's development: the larger they get, the more they eat, and the older they get, the more they need to know. We need to sketch an outline and begin a discussion that draws people out. We need to sit down with each other, with a trust and an agreement between us. We need to realise how much we don't know, while prophesying to each other with what we do know. Don't be in a rush for knowledge: true knowing is very costly and too many accumulated facts are detrimental to mental health. The more we engage the creation, the more we will come to know and share and agree together on. The more we occupy the heavens as his body, the church, the greater our vantage point will be with regard to the created order. The more we love (speaking that love in truth and that truth in love), the more we will 'grow up in all aspects [things] into him who is the head' (Eph. 4:15), and the more we will come to know him who fully knows us.

Show me the method

How does this translate? So, you want a method, do you?

To speak plainly now (so you might perhaps think I am speaking from God!) I would suggest the following.

Do sketch an outline and do teach about the Hebrew vision of creation and the church as the fullness of him who came to fill all things, but don't offer closure and don't map it out in a method. In effect, speak it out and let the content sit there for a time, giving things time to stir up the good and the not yet good things within people. Let responses arise and then discuss them, leaving more things open; again, not rushing to closure. Of course you can do whatever you want, in that this 'non-method' method I am suggesting needs to suit your situation. What I am suggesting, however, is that truth be given time to leaven its way through, rather than being allowed to form its own sermon-series lump with bells, whistles, guarantees, buttons, methods, pseudo-arrivals and vision statements attached.

Let the level of growth call forth the level of conversation. Leave plenty of space for people's discovery, and then allow them to speak of what they have found. Ask more questions and give less commentary. Tell more stories and offer less direction. Jesus came to utter things that had been hidden since the foundation of the earth beneath our feet (Mt. 13:35). We need to tell of things as they are and stop projecting towards ideal arrival points that are not. This will ensure that the lines of sight and understanding in the Hebrew vision of the church will arrive in the saints' lives in creation, rather than on paper or in the pulpit only. Even though we might be frustrated at the time it takes for the new to appear, we need to allow God's time to do its work in us. Remember the accelerator principle that God has placed in the leaven of the Kingdom. Think about what one seed over several seasons can bring into being. Again, we are not talking about a go-slow programme; we are speaking of divine salt, light and leaven designed by God and well able, if treated with respect, to penetrate the world.

A good friend once asked me if I could get together several people who had gone through church transition and had had several years of teaching and experience in relation to the Hebrew way of being the church. I agreed, pleased that I would be able to showcase the many good things I had done. (If you are detecting pride here, you are right, so hold on for the fall.) We got the dinner thing out of the way and then, with coffee in hand, we began sipping and saying what the last number of years had meant. As we went round the room, no one mentioned me, no one spoke of my Hebrew teaching ministry, no one told of the great transition of '98. They all spoke of their life and their work, of the things they had found in God, of their sense of being the church wherever they were. I was waiting for some recognition but, by the time the table had been rounded, I still had none. It seemed that no one was aware of how much I had done.

As they got about half way round the table, it dawned on me why affirmation – at this critical time of trying to impress an overseas visitor – was not forthcoming. It was because the Hebrew vision of creation and the church was not some external thing to these people. It was not some plan or grid out there that they continually had to aspire too. Rather, the truth in the Hebrew vision had become intrinsic to them. It had become so normal to them that it was now merged, united, one with their day-to-day breath, sound and struggle. So, because no one was going to pat me on the back that night, I decided secretly and quietly to pat myself on the head. 'Well done,' I said to my frail male ego. If only they knew how successfully I had carried out my own planned obsolescence.

I realised that night just how much these people had been weaned off leaders, weaned off grids, weaned off methods – because they now had and held the substance for themselves. They had dug the wells and they now had access to their own water. Certainly, they still called for the power of agreement and for resources at times – but they were not dependent on me. They were not dependent on 'my' teaching ministry. They were not members of 'my' organisation any more. They were sons and daughters now grown and released to be the church as fullness. We have a responsibility as leaders in local church and church-at-work settings to teach what the Word says about God's world and God's church. Let us put in place that divine and Hebrew sketch. Let's use it to locate each other as members one of another; to locate our work as key to the divine strategy; to locate Christ as head over all things, and to locate the angels who guard and garrison all of our good work in Christ in creation. With the Hebrew sketch in place our map now looks like this:

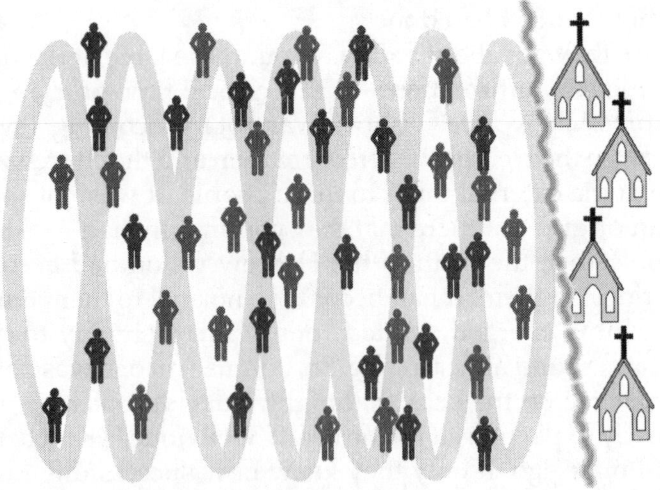

The elliptical lines represent the Hebrew language and worldview, enabling the saints to better locate themselves and each other in the creation as Christ's body, the church.

Time now to add some parables to the canvas.

10

Painting Parables on the Canvas

James

Jesus, to put it simply, spoke in parables. The master teacher, the creator of all things – including cognitive and learning processes – told lots of stories. These parables both revealed and concealed divine truth. Because of this, they were chosen to be the main teaching vehicle of the hidden mysteries and open revelations of the emerging Kingdom: good enough for Jesus – good enough for us. Every parable Jesus told was an account of how things happen, whether it was a story about a small seed becoming a large tree, or about a father first losing and then regaining his son. As such, parables are able to combine all the elements of truth – the concept, morality, the relational – all in tension and interrelated in the one narrative.

This is in contrast to the more rational and Platonic way of thinking, which is reductionist. The Platonic approach reduces the elements of life into bottles, labelling each one by name for separate and singular examination. This causes the rational dimension of truth to become exaggerated and dominant over, and often against, all other aspects of what is true. Over time, this way of approaching reality often renders people unable to relate the different parts of their life together again. Sounds like a nursery rhyme about an egg, does it not?

The Kingdom was very hard to communicate in one, two or even many sittings to the farmers and shopkeepers of Jesus' day. Likewise, the Kingdom is very hard to communicate in words to mobile phone users of today. That is why Jesus would often say 'the Kingdom of heaven is like … .' He did this to communicate the heart of the Kingdom, to give people a taste of what it looks like. He did this so that they would recognise the Kingdom as it emerged in and from the midst of their lives, their works and their faith. As Jesus did this, he invited enquiry, he revealed hearts and he established truth coordinates for eternal life. Through the parable, Jesus issued an invitation for people to align the good in their own heart to those qualities, truths and strengths that were the heartbeat of the Kingdom.

Of course, preachers tell lots of stories, and this enables them to communicate truth more effectively. However, even though parables are used as a teaching technique in the church as construct, the main parable communicated ends up being the church itself. Most stories told tend to be about what the pastor is thinking, feeling and doing. More often than not they are about conferences, church ministries and moves of God in other churches. These parables, so powerful in communicating truth, are told inside the church building during the weekly service. It's hardly surprising that we have so effectively trained the saints to see the church gathered in the building as the key container for the divine person and purpose on earth.

We have an opportunity before us to change that, and to do so we will need to redeploy the parable. The living and working parables on the landscape are the greatest cultural accelerators we have. The good works they speak of are the ones that God prepared for us from before time began. This is why good works are emphasised so often in the New Testament. In chapters five and six we looked at the power and place of our good works, of the light they shine, of the inheritance they gather, and of the creation mandate they express and enable us to fulfil. It is our work that tells us who we really are.

Our work combines all that we are and expresses it to others and to the creation. Truth, love, motivation, gifting, dysfunction, fear, pride, hope, desire – the list of things we bring to work is long and very real. God created work, not just because it helps supply the money we need to function, but so that we would know who we are, so that we would engage with the earth and each other and thereby gather our eternal inheritance. Our creator gave us work so we would come to know him in and through the fruit of our good work (Col. 1:10). Apostolic, prophetic, evangelistic, pastoral or teaching ministries do not lead the charge into the new landscape. It is the good works of the saints in every sphere of creation that have that right and have that capacity. Let's look at one such living and working parable now occupying ground as the church as fullness.

A man, a woman, a good desire and a city

I might as well introduce this parable in a scriptural way. The Kingdom of heaven is like two friends of mine, a man and woman, married with two children who are now grown. The fellow is from a consultancy and banking background and the woman has trained and worked in social work. God had created and ignited their heart to establish a place where leaders in the different spheres of work in the city could come and spend time talking about the things that mattered. They were moved by good desire to create a setting where heads of corporations, people in small or medium businesses, heads of universities, politicians, college lecturers, artisans and those working with street kids, Christian and not, could gather together. As these people gathered, they could talk about the disturbance they felt concerning the way things were. They could dialogue about the vision their heart once held before economic rationalism came and crushed it. They could commune with people who still felt that something worthwhile could be salvaged from the mad rush for status and money. They could agree together to make a difference.

The place they purchased is great. It's a well-appointed property with a house designed by a well-known Australian architect. It's the kind of place that leaders in the city like to visit, away from the concrete and the bottom line, but not too far away. The price these two paid, both financially and personally over years of preparation and prayer, to see this place rise from the earth was great. All that they had was put on the line. The fellow told me of the day that he first headed into the city to present his manifesto to business leaders. The place and property were ready to go. He and his wife were ready to go. An outline of the way in which diverse groups of leaders might exchange, converse and agree together for change, Camp David-style, over two days of conversations was now ready to present. Because of his history in the city, the fellow had no trouble getting his first set of appointments. The day came; he got dressed for the city, and then with papers in his suitcase and faith in his heart he headed into the city. His wife waved him off. Five days later he would return.

Through the lobby, up in the lift to the smiling reception desk. Waiting . . . then the solid wooden doors of power open. He walks in. 'Hello.' 'Hello to you,' comes the reply . . . and he begins to speak of his desire, drawn from the deep over many years of fire, to the harried person on the other side of the desk. My friend was prepared, not with some set piece, but by thirty years spent in the city, seeing, working and praying in its heart.

He opened the batting by speaking of the disturbance in the city, of the drift from the things we value to the things that bring harm to us, to our families, to the nation, of the need for courageous leadership at this time. The response to his proposal was pretty much the same in every one of the next five encounters. The person on the other side of the conversation blinked, looked puzzled, discreetly checked their watch, called to mind their bottom line and politely said thanks, good idea, but no thanks. Some of them did agree in part, and in principle, with elements of what was said, but were at a loss to work out just what my friend wanted to sell them.

After appointment number six and three days had passed, my friend walked out onto the street below the office that had just smiled him off. The sky was overcast and when it saw him, it decided to rain. So wet, unembraced by anyone in the towering offices above, his burden and heart unreceived by those he had a burden and heart for, the fellow began to feel pain. This pain was his dying, but also his turning point and a turning point for many. Let's not get ahead of ourselves here. In the wet street, the pain collided in him, hitting him with the 'I must be stupid' wave of emotion (so acute for the male of the species in particular). The feeling of being stupid was then compounded by the money thing – the very thing that the city was built to make. You have spent it all on this and no one wants it. The fellow opened his black umbrella against the sky, and went off to visit number seven.

As he entered through another set of solid wooden doors with the feeling of death now on him, there came to him a freedom from fear that only close encounters with death can bring. He felt a new liberty simply to share his heart, come what may. As he spoke, the eyes of the fellow who listened began to glisten just enough to encourage our saint to keep going and believe even more in what he was saying. When his set of frail words was complete and the gap between the two men fell into silence, their eyes talked awhile. In that moment, something happened to change the course of things for many. The man in charge of so much told the saint with the delicate desire that what he had heard was something he had been waiting a very long time for someone to say. He knew it, but could not articulate it, let alone share it at the shareholders' meeting. Now someone had turned up, not to sell a widget, but to walk alongside him, to join with his created heart, to speak into and about the things that are true and to do this right there in the heart of the city.

Seven years on, hundreds of people from key places of power and influence have come together in this place to spur each other on to do the things of worth; to engage in real and courageous leadership that changes things for the good. A shared culture has formed between many. A power of agreement between saints and many who are not saints but still love truth has emerged. So many thousands of conversations about life, about Christ, about what matters have taken place. So many things that cannot be measured, so much good, so much struggle and so much light has been given to a city in darkness. The Kingdom of heaven is like this man and this woman and their good work. This man, this woman and their work are the church. Of course, they don't have the name 'church' on a sign on their fence, they have it in their hearts and in the agreement they share with others. It's a name given to them by Jesus Christ and they dare not let go of it on their journey towards and through the gates of the city they love.

There are so many things that can be drawn from this parable, so many things that remain unsaid. Here I draw out just a few. A culture is emerging from this place that many saints and many who are not saints are identifying with. They are gathering, they are sharing resource, they are talking and working through the issues that matter. Emerging Christian leaders gather from time to time to speak about how to survive in the new economy: about when and how to make a stand against what is not good in your corporation; about working with old economy managers and with people from other cultures; about when to fight for change and how not to fall, martyr-like, on your own sword by moving too early in the piece. They are agreeing, they are building, they are being the church and making their mark in the city.

Secondly, from the very start this expression of Christ's body, the church, is growing alongside and integrated with the culture of those who are not Christians. This good work, salted by Kingdom salt, undergirded by prayer, garrisoned by angels and in possession of the name 'church', is not separated from the culture of the city – it is growing up together with it. One might think, in line with certain Scriptures, that such would dilute its culture or taint it. This could, of course, happen to any work of this nature or, for that matter, to a local church or 'ministry'. I am not saying that the good work this parable speaks of is exempt from such a tendency. What I am saying is that separation into a sub-culture is no guarantee against infection. As one friend of mine observed, 'Jesus said we should be in the world and not of it. Not only are we, as the church, not in the world, we have become isolated in a church sub-culture from it. And inside that sub-culture we have become worldly: increasingly demanding this and that to keep us happy, fed, entertained and coming along.'

My observation has been that the proximity of this parable to the city has had a major influence in keeping its good desire focused and growing. It has a much stronger capacity for reality checks and balances than most local churches I have been involved with or observed. This is because the world, the creation and the people around us are the main measure of who we are as Christ's body, the church. Remember that Jesus came into the world for sinners. Remember that the whole of creation cries out for the sons and daughters to come and liberate it from its bondage to decay. Remember that our eternal inheritance is found in the cities, in the spheres of creation and in relationship with the people therein. Platonic thinking has caused us, as the church, to locate reality away from this life. It has taken away so much of our vision of God and his purpose in, through and over the creation. The new landscape church does not grow up inside a building; it grows up in the 'all things' (Eph. 4:15) of creation. Rather than this causing the church as fullness to falter, it causes the body, the church, to know where it stands in regard to the heaven and the earth.

One Lord, one faith, one baptism

Imagine in five years' time in, say, Germany or France, a culture of being church emerging: one that needs no building or name to define and hold it. Rather than the newer denominations going into Europe and spending twenty years building just another form of congregation-centred church, one that is deemed to be sectarian and foreign to much of European culture, we have the capacity to build something integrated from the start. As we saw in that accountancy practice, there is scope to see those from Catholic, Lutheran, charismatic and Baptist traditions join as one body in the good work, to be salt, light, leaven and church. We do not have to expend all of that time and energy dislocating people from their culture, trying to get them to join in our particular brand of meeting or denomination. This culture, this way of church, will also emerge alongside those who have no identification with a Christian tradition. These people will no longer have to jump mountains and valleys to relate to the church, because that church, that body will be working alongside them, gathering, praying, resourcing, redeeming work and thereby drawing them to the light that it shines in the place where light so needs to shine. This is not a dream, it's now happening. It was Bonhoffer who said that organised religion – the church – was the greatest hindrance to Christianity coming to a Europe that has had enough of it. He advocated, in his short but intense life, a 'religionless' Christianity. We have, I believe, sufficient sight, desperation, wisdom and permission to be and build that church at this time.

So many parables are emerging on the landscape that there would not be time enough to tell them. There are accounts from the factory floor as well as the executive chair; from the family home as well as the AA meeting. These have been going on, of course, in different measure since time began. They are not something that has only arisen in the past ten years. What is different is that they are now becoming more visible than they have been. The reason for this is that more of these parables are taking the name 'church' to themselves. They are taking permission to be at the forefront of the Kingdom move into creation. They are building from the good desire of heart and will no longer be stopped or tied by authority structures that set limits on their reach into creation.

They don't want to be in an adversarial relationship with leaders of local church settings, but for far too many years they have been waiting for real permission to come from them. They are now drawing permission from each other and from society to do the good works and be the church they are and always have been. Rather than them coming back into some ecclesiastic church line, local church leaders themselves need to come back into line by joining with and serving these Kingdom parables now multiplying in the land. These parables are not the extension of the church of elsewhere: they are the church, the fullness of the one who came to fill all in all. These good-working parables are the heart of the emerging church as fullness. They carry the culture and they create the culture of the new landscape.

With the sight lines of the Hebrew vision of the church now drawn, we can paint the parables onto the canvas before us. In the following and third graphic, I will use the Star of David motif to signify such parables. This star is used in the business model from Sykes that I have mentioned, and suggests a different way of work than that which has arisen from the hierarchical, pyramid-like structures of the world system.

The lines of sight that the Hebrew vision of the church as fullness brings enable us to begin to see each other's lives and works for what they are in God's purposes. As mentioned previously, these are not the back foot of the Kingdom; they are the front line of creation engagement. The more the power of agreement rises between these people and their works, the more partnership, sharing of resource, gathering, resource of ministry gifts and strength from mentoring elders will join with the powerful name 'church' to prevail against the gates of hell in every sphere of creation engaged by our good work.

Because these good-working parables are the key to occupation and culture acceleration, we will be looking at them again from different perspectives as we cover

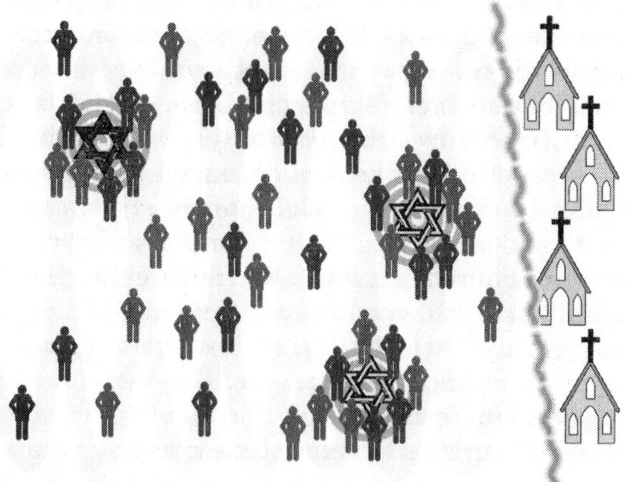

the resource, pioneers, gathering and order phases of culture-building in the new landscape. Here I include a quote that summarises, in part, the ground we will be covering. It is from the book *The Church Beyond the Congregation*.

Right now, there are multiplied tens of thousands of businesses established by saints in the spheres of the created order engaged by work. Many of the saints who work in these businesses desire to see them built on Kingdom principles. In a post-modern world, where society relates mostly to what is useful, tangible and workable, there is a tremendous opportunity for these workplaces to become the front line of our engagement of creation as the church. Once leaders take hold of the truth that the church can exist in every sphere of life, they can with confidence and wisdom begin to serve those who are that church.

Increasingly we are seeing what might be called 'redemptive structures' coming into being. These businesses seek out the purposes of God in the sphere of creation they engage, with a view to bringing substantial restoration to that sphere. In these settings, a relationship (either paid or unpaid) is established with an individual who is a ministry gift of Christ. He or she works (serves) to see the believers involved in the business encouraged, equipped and resourced for more effective ministry. The people who operate and work in these businesses seek to establish powerful relational networks that radiate from their place of work. All of this is done with a view to shining light and bringing salvation to the lives of those who engage the services and/or purchase the products of that business. Missions, particularly in places within the 10/40 window, are increasingly using such an approach in an endeavour to penetrate and impact societies with the Gospel. If it's good enough for the field, then it surely must be good enough for our own increasingly unreached society. (P.260)

The Kingdom of heaven is also like a factory

One more parable before we head off to look at resource. This one comes from Sheffield, England, from a salt of the earth fellow by the name of Jim Bancroft. When we speak about the body of Christ working in the spheres of creation, some get concerned that this may lead to elitism, with only entrepreneurs and corporates getting a look in. Among many other tremendous things touched on by this parable is the way in which it speaks of Christ's body, the church, emerging from the factory floor. The events covered in this account happened around thirty years ago. In this story, many of the things that we will be covering ahead, and many of the areas of concern you might now be experiencing from reading the book thus far, are touched on or triggered – hence the length of it. It's a most amazing account: one that has been hidden for so long because it was a parable without a culture to keep its life, its story and ultimately its work alive.

> I worked for an engineering company in Sheffield, England, which made clutches, overdrives for cars, and certain garage equipment. The company had about 1,200 employees. My job at the company was a 'setter' and what I used to do was 'set' machines up or operations on machines for operators to command the machines and do a good job. At that particular time, the company was very union-oriented (as were a lot of companies at that time). The union had an iron grip on the company and everybody who worked there had to pay subs to the union every week. The union did do some good things, don't get me wrong, but they did do some silly things, because they had too much power.
>
> Where I was based in the factory, there were two Christians. One was a very keen Christian and the other was a fairly keen Christian, but not quite as keen as the other one. This was because he kept on witnessing to his wife and tried to get her to go to church. She told him to cool it or she would go back to her mother. And so, from then on, he had stopped going to church. He played a big part in my becoming a Christian, even so. The other lad was a more regular churchgoer. Lunchtimes were great times. We used to play cards or dominoes. These two Christians used to sit and read the Bible and discuss it. I became very curious about what they were doing. I'd had a church background, in that I had always been in Sunday school, the Cubs, Boys' Brigade, the Scouts and the youth club, so I didn't feel embarrassed to talk to them. I spent some time talking to them about the Bible and I came up with some very good arguments, because I knew my Bible stories. There was one thing that they shared more than once that I couldn't get my head around and that was their own personal testimonies of how they had become

Christians. I didn't have an argument for that because it was their own personal experience.

God began to speak to me around the time my girlfriend's father died. We used to spend a lot of time together working on our cars and I used to get along with him well. I had not been touched by any death on my side of the family so it hit me in a big way. God started to speak to me more and more through that. At that time, God seemed to be in everything I did or said. I would look at the stars, and the wonder of creation made me think about God. I went to the coast for a day or so, and seeing the sea made me think about God. I went to the country and God spoke to me, and I got to the point where there was nowhere to turn, everywhere God was prompting me to make a decision. I felt the Lord say 'Jimmy, it's time to make a decision. You're at the point of no return: repent and ask me into your life.'

One day, when I got up early for work, I felt a bit weird. It felt as if it was going to be a 'different' day that day. It was while I was at work setting up a machine and operating it that God started to speak to me very strongly and I knew I had to make a decision – I couldn't hold out any longer. So I stopped the machine right there, and on the spot I prayed, repented and asked God into my life.

I went around immediately telling everyone on the shop floor. I was so excited, and although some people didn't agree with what I was saying or didn't understand what I was saying, they could see my excitement. People were saying 'Look, we don't know what's happened to Jim but something has happened to him.' Within a few days or so, a dozen of my friends and colleagues had become Christians, and from then on there was someone saved every single day. It didn't just stay in the factory but spilled out outside, because our girlfriends, wives, parents, brothers, sisters and cousins all started to become Christians. My wife became a Christian, and so did her sister. Since then, my wife has probably helped lead thousands of people who came from the factory to Christ.

All we had to share with people was our testimony, because we didn't really know the Bible. We didn't know anything about the Holy Spirit. All we knew or had heard of was God. A friend of mine at the time said 'Jim, I don't understand this – it's like a massive wave of God over which we have no control, no control at all.'

We felt that it was quite important to learn a bit more about the Bible, and found out about something that was called the 'Topical Memory System', from which you would get Bible verses through the post on little cards to memorise. So, each day we would get our memory verse and stick it on our machine, on the workbench or drawing board, and we would learn it. Then at lunchtime we would test each other and discuss what we had learnt that day, what we had learnt that week and what we had learnt over the past few weeks and months. So we learnt a lot of the Bible and it did help us in our witnessing.

Each person discipled another person. I had someone disciple me and I would disciple another, so that everybody was discipled by somebody else. There was much to do in the evenings because that's when we would do the discipling. We were happy to be so busy, because we were doing what God wanted us to do.

It was getting very exciting at work now. I can't explain the experience of work – it was absolutely incredible. There were a lot of us by now, so the company gave us the boardroom to meet in to have prayer in the mornings and Bible study in the evening. Actually, we had our Bible study as soon as work finished at 4.30 p.m., so we didn't go home until after it had finished.

We started to print our own magazine and put testimonies in it. These were very relevant, because they were read by guys who were working next to the guys who had their testimonies in there. We used to put in tips on things like gardening, fishing and cooking, which people found really useful. The company bosses gave us permission to be at the gate five minutes before everybody else, so that we could go outside with big cardboard boxes full of newsletters to give out. Everybody used to take one, because the topics in there were the topics of discussion on the shop floor for the rest of the week. We never found any on the floor – that's incredible, isn't it? Everybody used to take them.

We prayed every morning. I used to get up at about a quarter to five. All sorts of people were saved, from labourers to managers: no grade was excluded. All the 'girly' calendars came down and the company let us put Christian posters up. Also, the toilets were repainted to cover up all the rude jokes and pictures. Christians took over all the positions of shop stewards, because there were so many of us now. So, as all the shop stewards were Christians, there were no more strikes.

About half of the workers at the company became Christians. Production levels went up by 60 per cent, because we were working harder, and scrap levels came right down. The ceiling was taken off the bonus earnings and our bosses doubled our wages overnight without us even asking, because we were doing so well.

The company began to supply free overalls and free safety wear. They built us a sports club, tennis courts, bowling green and children's area. This was the new environment God had created for us to work in. The company started a fishing club, a cricket club, arts teams, cycling teams, a bowling club, archery and football clubs and probably others that I can't remember as well. They even organised and paid for day trips to the coast for all the families. We began to get sent work from other factories within the group because we were so efficient. The company built the finest training centre for apprentices in the country and, in fact, the finest in Europe

> (although I must be modest). The company took over our magazine: they produced it and paid for it and it went out with our wages. You couldn't get your wages without getting one of our magazines.
>
> We decided to send people out to churches because there were so many of us and we thought we should get them to church. I suppose we were already a church in our own right, but because the church had no influence in what God was doing we started to get people into churches in the area, in the city where they lived. Unfortunately, the church didn't seem to appreciate what God had done and told us that they should have been saved at church and not at work. But we carried on trying to get people integrated into churches. This caused many problems, but that's another story.

This account touches on it all – the work, the witness, the discipling, the accountability, the restoration, the families, the financial blessing, the struggle between the church as fullness and the church as construct. What Jim was politely saying in relation to the church as construct was that once the churches in the area began to enter into the move of God it became confused, got political, and over time it was stopped. God forgive us!

The Kingdom of heaven is like a man by the name of Jim Bancroft. It's time for tens of thousands of saints like him to be seen, known, encouraged, trusted and equipped to be the church – the fullness of him who fills all in all. People like Jim didn't need controlling, they needed serving. They are the leaders of the new and we, as ministry gifts and elders, are their followers. Heaven is ever looking for people like Jim. God is after you; he knows the works he has prepared beforehand for you to do. He knows where you work and was there before you got the job. Next time you're standing under the night sky, tilt your head heavenward and listen for God to say 'Is that you, my son? Is that you, my daughter? Let's together good-work this place into eternity.'

In the emerging church as fullness, teaching ministries can help but do not lead the way; apostolic teams can serve but do not lead the way; intercessors can prepare but do not lead the way. It's people like Jim and the couple engaged with leaders in the city who make the way. The new landscape church is not characterised by its leaders; it is not distinguishable because of its meetings or buildings – it is known by its people and made manifest through their good work in every sphere of creation. Let's now look at how these good-working parables, growing under God's good heaven, fuelled by the power of agreement, can be resourced in such a way that they are served, but not swamped.

11

Resources From Heaven

James

As the good-working parables begin to grow, both in themselves and in numbers, they begin, like anything that develops, to hunger for more resource to fuel their increase. This fuel includes things like more staffing, finance, strategic planning and the like. In a good-working parable there will also be the call for more input from the Word of God. This hunger for truth and resource is of course there all the time, but there are times of greater need and thus greater hunger. Many are the resources of God for our life and work, and they include such things as staff and finance as well as truth from his Word. In this chapter, I will be focusing in particular on the role and resource supplied by the ministry gifts of Christ. As we shall see, these saints are called to minister the truth of God in a unique way to the body of Christ.

As parables grow and multiply, they draw forth more ministry gifts to assist them in their good work. Hence the mention of these gifts of Christ at this stage of progression in the new landscape culture. Another reason why the ministry gifts are emphasised here is because if they enter into the landscape in bulk too early in the piece, before the parables have developed sufficient momentum, they might tend to dominate the process with old models of ministry. The current approach to ministry concentrates more on words than it does on works: and the works it does emphasise are often those done by the ministry itself. If too many ministry gifts come on too strong with an old way of operating, they will tend to eclipse the frail and emerging works of the saints. Again, they need to have a border check before they cross over into the new landscape, taking off their boots before they enter so as to tread carefully in and around the good works now in progress in the garden.

As mentioned in Chapter 9, 'New Landscape Language', truth does not arrive all at once but is given to us as it is needed for the journey. As this wisdom comes from above, it does not eclipse or replace our own store of wisdom. Rather, it weaves in with our life to help us draw more of the good and more of the inheritance from our work. When we agree on earth concerning the work before us, heaven responds by sending more resources our way. I stress these two things here because it helps us to get a feel for what ministry gifts are meant to be and do. Firstly, they express or supply more of heaven's resources, in response to the level of agreement and good work we have attained on earth. Secondly, they come to add to and further equip these works, rather than being sent to manage or lead them.

Before we take a more in-depth look at these ministry gifts, I need to stress that there are many other areas from which resources for the saints come – prayer, family, friends, colleagues, old hymn books, walks in the country and so on. These ministry gifts sit in and among all that God has given us pertaining to life and godliness. One more quick point. As we consider the role of ministry gifts it is important to know that they are not only to be found inside local churches, they have been strategically positioned by God in the church as fullness in every sphere of creation. Our challenge is that, to date, we have not been given the sight we need to see and value them. Let's dip back into the book of Ephesians and read from chapter 4:

> Therefore, it says, 'When he ascended on high, he led captive a host of captives, and he gave gifts to men.' (Now this expression, 'He ascended,' what does it mean except that he also had descended into the lower parts of the earth? He who descended is himself also he who ascended far above all the heavens, *so that he might fill all things*.) And he gave some as apostles, and some as prophets, and some as evangelists, and some as pastors and teachers, for the equipping of the saints for the work of service, to the building up of the body of Christ; until we all attain to the unity of the faith, and of the knowledge of the Son of God, to a mature man, to the measure of the stature which belongs to the *fullness of Christ*. (Eph. 4:8–13 [Italics mine])

Notice the way in which the ministry gifts in this passage are placed between the mention of Christ's plan to 'fill all things' and the call on the body to be his 'fullness'. As such, they are portrayed as being pivotal to the divine purpose. Also notice, as I have already mentioned, that they come as a gift package from the risen Lord situated in heaven above us. What are these gifts from heaven? They are people. What kind of people? Some are apostles, some are prophets, some are evangelists and some are pastors and teachers. We are accustomed to seeing these people operate from a pulpit in a church or conference. This is a part of what many of them do, but here we want to place the emphasis more where Paul, in Ephesians, places it. That place is the creation context rather than a congregational one. Paul's focus is the works of the saints in that creation, rather than the ministry of the preacher in the gathered church.

In that good-working creation context, what do these ministry gifts get up to?

Anointed to equip, called to serve

Each one of these five gifts is anointed in a special way to minister a facet of Christ's person to his body, the church. They are able to impart or convey to us the attributes of Jesus – those he drew upon to accomplish the works he did on earth. Because we are made in God's image, the same qualities and attributes of the man Christ Jesus are also in us. Each ministry gift is called and enabled by God to activate and draw out the corresponding quality or attribute in our lives. If they are apostles they are given to draw out what is apostolic in us. If they are prophets they are called to activate the prophetic in our lives and so on. This is why they are so well suited to equipping us for the work of service (verse 12). They are able to speak into our lives, carrying in their words the agreement and resource of heaven. They help to ignite the things in us that we need if we are to operate in line with the level of creation engagement we have reached. They help to join our apostolic capacity to that of Christ. They help to fuel our abilities to teach, prophesy and nurture with the wisdom, fire and love of Jesus himself. They direct, in a unique way, heaven's agreement to ensure that what is done in heaven is done in our own lives and works on earth.

Ministry gifts can at times be used by God to break ground, particularly when it comes to the initial entry of the Kingdom into a city or region. This is seen in the apostle Paul's ministry, when he encountered a new city untouched by the Gospel of the Kingdom. Like Paul, once the initial ground is broken, the ministry gift needs to step back and equip the saints to occupy the ground that has been taken and, from there, resource and encourage them to take further ground in every sphere of creation in the city. Paul's ultimate purpose was to create an apostolic church in the cities he impacted. To instil this attribute into the character of the church in the city, he first patterned it by word and deed. Then he drew back by moving on, creating space and giving permission to the body to follow his example and become, over time, the apostolic soul-winning people God wanted them to be. Leadership by elders and ministry gifts follows this pattern. It is intermittent, rather than constant. It comes on strong, sets in place a pattern, lays down some coordinates and then moves off stage. The space then invites the saints to enter in and occupy by writing their own script and doing their own works. As soon as the ministry gift can, he or she needs to step back, coming alongside the saints to equip them to take the initiative and occupy. It is this ebbing and flowing way of ministry that, I believe, we need to get a sense of at this time.

Most of the current leadership approach tells us that ministry gifts need to get out ahead of the saints and keep ahead, so that there will be someone strong and visionary for them to follow. This makes its mark initially, in that people will generally respond more readily to something strong and clear. However, over time, the record shows that passivity, uniformity and dependence are usually the result of such leadership. Strong leaders who are relentless in their leadership do not create strong people, they create weak people.

Is the answer, then, to have weak leaders? No. To my mind, we need leaders who know how to ebb and flow. Leaders need to weave in and serve the saints as their need and hunger require. They need to be good stewards, who give the saints food at the proper time (Mt. 24:45) and do not overfeed them. At times they will be strong and then they need to go weak. At times they are present and then they will need to absent themselves, giving space for choice and time for truth to mix with desire to make the good work. They need to learn to dance, knowing when to lead and when to follow, but all along resisting the urge to become the DJ or manager of the club.

This approach to ministry is hard to integrate into our current culture and understanding of church. This is because we are accustomed to leaders managing a church centre and directing the Kingdom culture and works from that place. Because of this, teaching keeps coming every Sunday, leadership has to be exercised week-by-week and ministries of the church need to be managed month in and month out. If leaders in these situations stop teaching, leading or managing, they will be deemed incompetent and will soon be encouraged to seek other employment. Hence the need to see transition come to our way of being and building the church. Let's spend some time in the passage quoted above and dig down further into the nature and purpose of these gifts of Christ.

An invitation list for the good-working party

The list from Ephesians has a ring to it: apostles, prophets, evangelists, pastors and teachers – the kind of group you might want to take home to meet your mother (or perhaps not). It is hard to imagine these gifts of the risen Lord functioning in a different way to that which we have seen, but I believe that we need to start doing so. The church as fullness is in great need of these resources of heaven. When we start to try and see these ministries differently, our definition of them will get fuzzy for a time, before the shape of the new begins to emerge. (I hope that this statement will be of help in the confusion I am about to bring you!)

The focal point of the work of the ministry gift is to equip saints for the work of service. This perspective helps us to understand more about the actual nature of their role or function. We have tended to see them as gifted and anointed people who do sacred or supernatural things like prophesy and break ground in the Spirit, teach and preach the Word with conviction and power, conduct crusades that win the lost and the like. Again, ministry gifts are called to do things like these, but we have tended, as it were, to tip the balance this way because of our emphasis on the pulpit rather than on the day-by-day work of the saint.

If the prophet is called to equip the saint for their work in health, how are they going to do that? Is it only by prophesying to them at special times? I don't believe so. If this were the case, the saint slugging it out in health would become over-dependent on the anointed prophet to get the word he or she needs from heaven. When we trace the origin of these gifts, we locate them in Jesus Christ. He worked on the earth, and when he was about to head off to heaven he said 'The works that I do, you shall do also.' Then, as he ascended, he anointed the ministry gifts so that they could equip the saints to do these works. The point in having ministry gifts is all to do with the works of the saints, not the works of the ministry gifts.

It follows from this that the prophet is meant to communicate something of Christ (not just something from Christ) to the saints. This can, as mentioned, be a distinct word. But more than that, if the ministry gift is to enable us to do the good works, then he or she must impart something that conveys to us a capacity or power to get the job done. If we accept this we are faced with two options. This 'something' is either a purely supernatural capacity that is directly of God and does not connect with our own capacities, or it is a divine resource that works with and in us to enable us to do the works that God prepared for us. I would argue for the second. The prophets are not just called to prophesy, they are called to release the prophetic in every saint so that their works (and their words) testify of Jesus, who is the very spirit of prophecy (Rev. 19:10). In this way, we can see how the ministry gift in the person corresponds to the equivalent capacity in the saint. When we do this we can, I believe, bring them together into the kind of relationship that God intended. Those in ministry have for too long stood apart from the saints, both declaring the words and doing the works. It is time that they served the saints and equipped them to do the works that speak of divine life and reality. Let's now have a look at the different ministry gifts and the facet of Christ's ministering life that they communicate and convey from heaven to earth.

- **Apostle:** This gift of Christ speaks of breaking ground for the Kingdom. It activates in us that God-given capacity to press into more of life and more of work; to break ground in ourselves and in creation, that we might continue to grow, to occupy and to fill.
- **Prophet:** This expression of the risen Lord enables us to declare what is and what shall be. It triggers that capacity in us to see into what is and what is unfolding, to discern and draw out our own and others' desire regarding the people, the issues and the work before us.
- **Evangelist:** This good-news-telling gift enables us to win those we work with and relate to in life. It stirs that desire and gift within that wants to tell of the good things God has done, wants to declare his goodness in the land of the living. It stirs up our conviction to communicate with power the reality and truth of the Kingdom in which we are partakers.

- **Pastor:** This attribute of Jesus moves us to gather, care for and nurture others in such a way that healing and restoration comes to them and to the environments in which they live.
- **Teacher:** This anointing and enabling from God equips us to communicate to others in such a way that they come to know truth and are built up, changed and restored to the image of the God who made them.

The job description

Paul says that God gave some as ministry gifts. This would indicate that not everyone is a ministry gift, but rather that some are. These 'some' I will not try to identify, except to say that our definition of them as being 'full-time' local (or para) church-based ministries is far too narrow. As mentioned, these people are commissioned by God to express and convey, in a unique way, the different ministering capacities and qualities of the risen Lord to his body, the church. That being said, we all have a commission, in line with our own gifting and character, both to minister to others and to do the work God created us to do. The ministry gifts have a particular calling and anointing to concentrate more on the preparation, equipping and resourcing part of the divine process. These ministry gifts exist right through the church as fullness. You may well be one of the 'some'.

The job description of these expressions of Christ Jesus is given in chapter 4 of Ephesians. Again, it is essential that we place what we read here in the same context that the apostle Paul does. Quite clearly, the setting for what is taught here is the creation. What is in view in Ephesians is the body of Christ now standing between his head in the heavens and his feet on the earth: the one new man called to be the fullness of the 'all things' Christ Jesus ascended through and now desires to fill. No other context makes sense or does justice to what we read in chapter 4 of Ephesians. We have for too long placed these creation-encompassing truths concerning the saints, the ministry gifts and the divine purpose within the setting of the congregation. This placement has severely hindered the body in its calling to salt, light and leaven the earth. We can no longer afford such a strategic blunder. Let's look once again at the reason why God put ministry gifts into his divine equation for planet earth. It was 'for the equipping of the saints for the work of service, to the building up of the body of Christ; until we all attain to the unity of the faith, and of the knowledge of the Son of God, to a mature man, to the measure of the stature which belongs to the fullness of Christ' (Eph. 4:12–13). In the following chapter we will proceed to unpack this divine job description.

12

The Working Life of God's Equippers

James

We have tended to see the works of service referred to in Ephesians 4 as being mostly congregation-based, missionary, or charitable work. All of these settings can, of course, be places where good works happen, but with creation as our context, not only these works but also the saints' good work in the factory, the home, the office, the clinic and the classroom can come into view. What do the good works of the saints accomplish? The works of the saints combine to bring about the 'building up of the body of Christ'. The church as fullness is built not by congregations but by the saints good-working the creation towards the fullness. This is how Paul the apostle taught us to build the church. This is the pattern he laid down and, as he said in another epistle to another city, 'I laid a foundation . . . each man must be careful how he builds on it' (1 Cor. 3:10).

Teaching and gathering can help the body of Christ if they are part of an overall plan to be and build the church as fullness. If they are used to focus on the building of congregations, to my mind and in my observation, they end up working against, rather than for, the divine purpose. That is not to say that good things don't happen in these settings or that God does not bless the works and the gatherings in these places. What is in view in the above comment is that a preoccupation with this expression of the church (one that sees it as central rather than servant) ends up limiting the overall impact of individual saints with regard to their works in creation. This is because the congregation focus eclipses that work, and uses up most of the energy, resource and affirmation in keeping itself and its own ministries going.

United we work

Ministry gifts work with the saints and help them come into a relationship with each other in the works they do. The kind of relationship that ministry gifts help to foster among the saints is distinguished by what Paul calls 'the unity of the faith'. Here is a key word indeed – 'unity'. Jesus said that if his people were one, the world would know that he lives. Unity, it appears, is a key Kingdom thing. Much has been said and done concerning unity in the past decades. This has been good, but for the most part, in line with our doctrine of church, it has been about getting congregations and their leaders together for meetings. Again, this is a good initiative, but I believe that it has not created the kind of unity of the faith that Paul is speaking of here. Why not?

The setting for this unity of the faith is the creation. This unity arises as the body is built up in creation through the good works of the saints in every sphere of life. Unity for Paul is 'the whole body, being fitted and held together by that which every joint supplies' (Eph. 4:16). It follows from this that unity can only be measured by the extent to which every member of the body supplies, resources and relates to other members concerning the works of service done in creation. If we were to measure unity by this standard, we would have to conclude that the body is experiencing very little unity indeed.

Most saints in their working life are dislodged and dislocated from each other. They have little or no idea of what it means to be the church in their place of work. They draw very little resource and truth from their ministry gifts in relation to their work. The outcome of this situation is a body fragmented and profoundly weakened. We need to redefine unity, no longer measuring it by meetings but by the works of the saints in the spheres of creation. Remember the concerns noted in Chapter 8 relating to the saints being given permission to go their own way and become the church in their own sphere of work? The fear was that the congregations would be scattered and unity would be lost. I will critique this ecclesiastic logic in more detail in the 'gathering' chapter. For now, I note the desperate need we have to see unity come in the places where the body of Christ actually lives, works and engages the gates of hell. The world, for the most part, still does not know that Jesus lives. The body of Christ is not one. We do not have a unity of the faith in the place where God intended us to have it. We do not have unity in the place where the people we are trying to reach actually live, move and have their being.

Where is the Son?

This next part of the job description of the ministry gift is, I believe, the crown of their work. They are called, Paul says, to bring the saints into a 'knowledge of the Son of God'. At the moment we do not have this vision. 'What?' you might respond to this statement. 'You're saying we do not have a vision of Christ. Surely not!' I do not believe that we have had the vision of Christ that Paul speaks of in Ephesians. We have had a knowledge and sight of the

Christ who came to earth and died on the Cross. We have had a vision of Christ now living in a spiritual and removed heaven situated in the afterlife, the one who will one day come again. We know about the Christ who lives in our hearts and we have been particularly well informed about the Christ who is present when we gather as a congregation in church. We do not, however, have the vision that God wants us to have; that being the one that incorporates all other visions, expressions and revelations of Christ. The overriding and all-encompassing vision of Christ is the one that sees him standing right now through every sphere of the present creation in his body, the church. This is the Son of God Paul speaks of in Ephesians.

If the Son of God stands in, through and over the 'all things' of creation; if he is head over his body, the church – a body called to be and become the fullness of him who fills all in all – then ministry gifts must give saints a knowledge of that Son and live to build that body. It's an imperative. We must not obscure this vision of Christ or it will have serious ramifications for the life and works of the saints. It is this vision of Jesus Christ as head over all things that is able to bring all of our works, our relationships, our desire, truth, gatherings, ministry gifts and more into proper relationship in the divine purpose. Without this vision of the Son over all that they do, saints are unable to place themselves in the present age. They are disconnected from each other, divided against life, confused as to the purpose of their work. I wish this were an exaggeration, but it is not.

If the head is obscured and dislocated from the life and work of the body, what other outcome could we expect? The Platonic fog has obscured the heavens overhead, causing us, as it were, to misplace Christ. This has left believers with a narrow and obscured vision of the Son of God in their marriages, in their families, in their relationships and in particular in their work. Thus their ability to correlate the personal Christ preached on Sunday with the creation they encounter every day of the week is, compared to what it should be, severely limited. We challenge them to turn their eyes upon Jesus so that the things of earth will grow strangely dim. But if we gave them the knowledge of the Son of God standing through the seen and unseen spheres of creation, rather than facing a dimly-lit earth they would see the creation light up with the knowledge of him.

Double jeopardy

If this dislocation of Christ from creation continues, the fullness we were redeemed to inherit will remain a long way off. Our world will remain cloaked in dense darkness, and the church's journey to cultural oblivion as the salt that lost its savour will continue unabated. Some may fear losing the clarity, comfort and apparent unity of a Sunday meeting, but what is at stake is so much larger than that. We so need a vision of the creation-encompassing Son of the living God at this time. It is the ministry gifts of Christ that are both doubly privileged to give that to the saints and, as Scripture says, doubly in jeopardy of judgement if they do not.

The ministry gifts equip the saints for the works. The works combine to build the body. The more the body works, the more it shares life and comes into unity. As it grows and unites, the Son of God, the head of this body, comes into clearer focus. The knowledge of him was there all along, encouraged and taught by ministry gifts and as part of the language between the saints. However, there is a difference between words and works. Paul says in Colossians that it is in the fruit of good work that we come into the knowledge of God himself (1:9–10). The more the works and the culture that encourages and intensifies them increase, the more visible the body standing in creation becomes. The more substantial this body, the stronger will be the sight and sense of Christ as head in the heavens. This is why (coming back to the passage from Ephesians) we now hear Paul speaking of the emergence of the mature man. Again, just so that we will not be in any doubt about the divine purpose to fill all things, Paul summarises the goal once more at the end of the job description. He says that this new man, the one formed by Jew and Gentile, is the body growing to 'the measure of the stature which belongs to the fullness of Christ'. This was the plan all along. This was the purpose from the beginning of time. This is what God told Adam to do and this is what we, in the last Adam, Jesus Christ, must now do.

How great the need to release the many ministry gifts from congregation-minding into serving the church as fullness. How strong the imperative to recognise the many unnamed ministry gifts now residing in business, in healthcare, in home settings, in education and so on. How great the opportunity there is now to train ministry gifts to work with the church gathered in its many and varied forms and also to stand with and equip the saints in their works as the church as fullness. Like Jesus and John the Baptist, we need these ministry gifts in the market place; we need them in the byways of business and in the hallways of education; in the clinics and wards. They are needed, not so much as chaplains who do the work of ministry, but as mentors, as friends, as Kingdom consultants, as human resource people, as teachers and communicators, networkers, scouts, servants, resource gatherers. In that place they have the divine go-ahead to extend the power of heaven's agreement, give the saints the knowledge of the Son of God; trigger the created gifts and traits in them; stirring and equipping them to do the good works that were designed from all eternity to fill all of creation.

The ministry gifts are able to work across the landscape. As such, they have the capacity for greater overall sight of that landscape and thus are able to help fashion the works of the saints into a greater work: into a greater expression of church and a greater manifestation of unity than any one ministry, any one movement, any one congregation or set of congregations could ever see emerge. Imagine if the congregational leaders in the town where Jim Bancroft lived had had this vision of the church as fullness and not the one they were trained to see in Bible College. Instead of rebuking him, trying to take control of what was happening and then fighting with each other to lay hold of more congregation members, they might have assisted him by first saying well done. Then they could have offered some help in teaching the new Christians. Also, they might have invited the families to come on Sunday to their buildings for worship and further fellowship. All of this could have been named with that great name – His Church. Let's now upgrade our graphic. By the way, the slightly paler characters standing near the good-working parables are ministry gifts.

Healthy workers

A group of Australian healthcare workers joined with other health workers from various nations (including India, Sri Lanka, Thailand and the Philippines) for a three-day gathering in Sri Lanka. It was a strategic gathering that saw Christian healthcare networks come together from across denominational divides in those nations for the first time in a long time – possibly for the first time

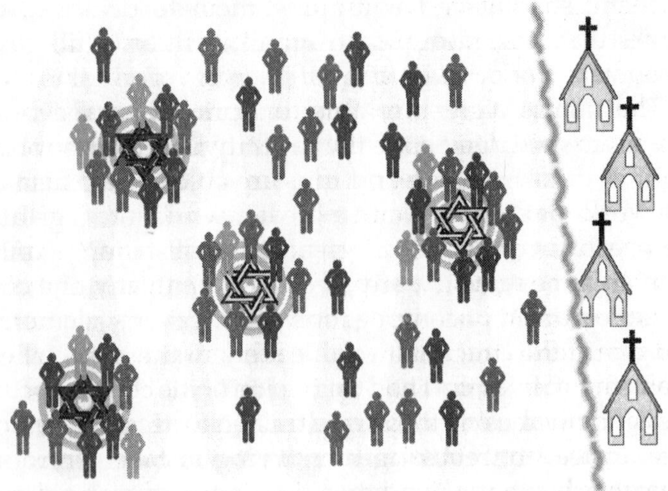

ever. The facilitator of the Australian contingent was a doctor friend of mine. I have worked with him as a ministry gift both in relation to Christian-run medical clinics and in relation to the broader network of healthcare workers that he serves with his wife and others. He contributed to the conference by speaking about the Hebrew worldview and the way of being the church and doing healthcare that arises from it.

When the three days were over, they decided that they would have a larger gathering the following year in one of the main Christian teaching hospitals in India. This would see a much larger network of healthcare workers representing tens of thousands of saints working in health coming together to build relationships and search out strategies for the way ahead. During the conference in Sri Lanka they were praying, seeking God that a new foundation for biblical healthcare and ministry in that sphere would arise to serve this new-found unity. The conviction was that this new foundation was to be the Hebrew vision of creation and of the church in all of life. The doctor had ignited something. Meanwhile, the ministry gift (me) was a long way away. What happened next is very important.

When the Australian contingent gathered for a debrief and future planning session, I was invited to join them. There were about fourteen people in all in that meeting. It was great to see these workers recount their experiences. We began to speak about next year's gathering in India and the feeling was, initially, that an internationally known speaker, a prophetic ministry gift, should come and minister to the newly gathered networks. We talked about the cost of that and, as we did, we began also to speak of the cost in Australia of getting well-known speakers in and the difficulty of getting enough people to come to make the conferences financially viable. We'd had to postpone a conference in an Australian city because of this problem. It was at this stage of my ebb and flow ministry that I decided to wade in more strongly.

I made reference to how much had been accomplished by a team of healthcare workers going to meet, pray and talk with other healthcare workers. I said that if, at this critical time in a new move in health in that region, they got in a 'big' speaker, a pattern would be established from the outset that might not put the right DNA into place for the future. If someone from elsewhere came with a powerful word, it might eclipse the words of others. It might cause people to think that the new move in healthcare and the basis of their relationship had more to do with that word from the prophet than with their own lives. I was not saying that speakers should never come and never prophesy; what I was challenging was the use of it as a default strategy to build the body, particularly after the process had already been initiated.

I then referred to our own situation in Australia, saying that we are in the same bind, in that unless we get in a known speaker, we don't think much will happen, and because of that we have less networking and gatherings of healthcare workers. I then suggested that we put aside a day or two, with some lead-up preparation, and meet to put together in our own words what we see God saying and doing in relation to healthcare at this time. I suggested that we then write it down and commit it to heart and memory and agree with each other to carry that communication out (in twos or threes) to groups around the nation. This would mean, I said, that when five people in a rural town want to commence a conversation, rather than sending a videocassette of a talking head to tell them the news, we could send two from this group to visit them.

One person then asked why they would want to listen to us. I said that they would listen because (as was the case in Sri Lanka) you came to them. Because of this, your time with them would have more to do with dialogue than monologue and you would be able to build stronger relationships with more people.

At this stage, the people around the table, who had begun to go somewhat passive at the mention of 'big' conference speakers coming to take over from what they had done, began to liven up again. One doctor to my left said 'I would love to do that – that's what I want to do – let's do it!' As you can see by the repetition of his phrases, this fellow would make a great communicator. I suggested that if we established this pattern, such a way of communication and impartation would be better able to travel down relational lines. It would also mean that we could multiply the language and networking more effectively, as we reached more places and commissioned and gave permission to others to do the same. We could take this to India next year and also see it happen there. The above is of course God's idea, summarised well by Paul in 2 Timothy 2:2. God had done a great thing in Sri Lanka, and ministry gifts and conference speakers could easily have got excited about it and wanted to move in strongly to have their say. But this move in the sphere of healthcare was about the saints and their work and, as such, it should remain about the saints and their work. A bit of help from a ministry gift is good. The relationship between doctor and ministry gift over many years was important, but the work and the inheritance in healthcare belong to this doctor and his fellow workers. Our inheritance as ministry gifts can only be realised as they gather their inheritance. In their inheritance is our inheritance.

Occupy till they come

So as you work, keep a look out for some ministry gifts. They might be in the next office, they might be the doctor in the next ward, they might be a Jim Bancroft, quietly but decidedly building up the body of Christ in and from the factory setting. If you are a ministry gift from an ecclesiastic setting and want to serve the church as fullness – go for it. As you enter the new landscape, don't do so as an extension of a church construct. To my mind, you don't even have to do it clothed in some ministry. Of course it's good to be in relationship and accountability, and if you need some tax vehicle to house what you do, then do so. But don't mistake your ministry vehicle for reality, don't confuse your heart desire with a vision statement that you then use to justify your right to be listened to. Be yourself, be in relationship, let the body call you forth. It's their turf that we are finally on now. We are no longer the managers of the work. We are their servants. Trust them, they are smarter than we think and will sort us out in no time!

When two or more agree on earth as touching any one work, then look out for the agreement of heaven. As a part of this agreement, look out in particular for a present from Jesus. He will gift-wrap some people and send them to serve and equip you for the work you have agreed with others to do. I know that many of these gift-wrapped ministry gifts have jumped out of their package and headed off to take care of congregations, but give them time, be patient. Draw on the ones that are around you now in your sphere of work. Ask God for an eye to see them and a nose to sense them. In the meantime and beyond that time, keep being and building the church as fullness with others; keep being apostolic, prophetic and the rest. By the time more ministry gifts are released onto the landscape, there will be, with your help, a culture of being the church that will help them acclimatise to the new workplace they find themselves in.

A quick note on pioneers

Like most topics, much more could be said in relation to pioneers. These people could have been listed along with good-working parables, and their works could in fact be named as pioneering parables. However, in view of our discussion regarding the ministry gifts and character traits of individuals in the body, I felt it important to leave mention of them until now. Pioneering is another way of saying apostolic. Pioneers are groundbreakers. The truth is that every saint has the capacity to break ground. Jim Bancroft was a groundbreaker.

What I am referring to here is people who, in their profession, are able to take significant ground, via discoveries, establishing new businesses, bringing significant cultural change to organisations and ways of doing work and so on. What marks these people as being apostolic is that they are able to break new ground in the sphere of creation they engage through their work. They are called to enter in as forerunners to the work and make a way for others to follow. They have been given the ability to see further into, and to pursue in a stronger manner, the unseen attributes, nature and power of God in the work they do.

Apostolic individuals generally travail more than others do. They are often not understood and are called 'maverick' and somewhat reckless. They often experience difficulty fitting into the present church culture. They make mistakes that others, who do not see, can take opportunity to disqualify them for. They are moved to ignite something; they are restless and vulnerable, strong-willed and weak. They are a mixture that no one can quite sum up. Whenever we are ready to occupy new ground, to rise to another level of glory in our journey to the heavens, God has his groundbreakers ready to perform that part of the good work.

My observation has been that as more parables emerge on the landscape, an environment is set in place that encourages more of these pioneering people and their works to emerge. It's as if a critical mass is formed, which propels the pioneers forward into the next level of breakthrough. These people have been working and breaking ground for some time, but the increase in the power of agreement and standing of the body is able to lift them into new places. As we are members of one another, this phenomenon is logical.

One thing that is sure about pioneering people is that, to this day, they are largely unaffirmed and unrecognised by pastors. They wait, along with the rest of the saints, in the spheres of creation, not for ministers to take charge of their work, but for ministry gifts to come and equip them for the good work. They need the ascension gifts of the risen Lord to come and help them attain to the knowledge of the Son of God now standing throughout the sphere of creation that they are called, as his body, to directly engage. These unlikely people hold an important key for this time. They have a God-given ability to penetrate the spheres of creation and make a way for the body to enter in to answer the cry. This capacity is found in their passion, their gifting and their strategic placement by God throughout his creation. We, as ministry gifts of Christ, need to find, serve and equip these individuals, together with all of the saints, for the eternal task given by God into both their and our own hands.

13

Unto Whom Shall the Gathering Be?

James

I was in conversation with two church leaders, when one of them said that they thought the best expression of church was for it to go monastic – a great turn of phrase, don't you think? The other fellow was an advocate of the cell model. He echoed the sentiments I read in one brochure advertising a cell conference that simply said 'Cell is it'. If another person had been there, she might have said that church for her was the traditional Sunday meeting in the building, where we are all together in God's house. It strikes me as strange that people who are the church are constantly trying to find out where church is and what form it should take. It's like a family who keep moving around the different rooms of their house trying to decide which one of the rooms is the family.

The logic is simple: if we are the church, then when we work we are that church, when we meet we are that church, when we sleep, take a meal with our family or have a coffee with our friends we are . . . wait for it . . . still the church. I know we know this, but in practice we tend, for the most part, to talk and act as if we don't. Those business people in the city praying like refugees were convinced that they were all members of the church of elsewhere. We have held the gathered church, under the wing of its leaders in a building or a house, to be the church proper and the church central. I remember speaking to one fellow who had been taught that the church was only the church if it gathered, because that's what he had been told the word *ekklesia* meant. I checked with him to make sure by asking 'So if you are not physically proximate to another member of your congregation, you are not church?' He stuck to his guns and so I asked one more question: 'Where does the church go when it's not meeting? Does it disappear? If so, it must be one of the weakest things on earth.' He had no answer. Your doctrine of church may not be that strict, but this demonstrates the kind of thinking that is out there. Hence the need to look again at what 'his church' is and is not.

We have made much of the word *ekklesia*; taking it to mean that the church gathered in a meeting is the central expression of church. This, to my mind, is not supported by Scripture. There was a church that gathered in the house of Apphia and Archippus (Phlm. 1:2) and that of Prisca and Aquila (Rom. 16:3–5). Most other references to the church being 'in' somewhere speak of cities; none speaks of buildings. When the word 'church' is defined in the key book of the church, Ephesians, it is not used to refer to a gathering; rather it speaks of the body of Christ in all of life and work in creation. An exception to this definition, one might think, is 1 Timothy 3:15, where the gathering of the church (as what Paul calls the household of God) is declared to be the church of the living God. Here, however, as was the case with the gathering in the houses of Aquila and Apphia, the church was first the church and then it gathered. The gathering did not make it the church.

Paul does use the name 'church' to refer to the gathering four times in 1 Corinthians, but such a usage, in the light of the rest of the New Testament treatment of the word *ekklesia*, cannot be used to construct a doctrine of church that says the gathering of itself is the primary and central expression of church. Here again, the church was first the church and then it gathered and hence it could take the name 'church' and apply it to the collective of people engaged in that activity. First came the church and then came its gathering, not the other way around. This is not an exhaustive study, but I would hope it serves to help us not to mistake that name, against which the gates of hell will not prevail, for the act of meeting. They are two distinct things with different meanings. It's only when we distinguish them that we will be able to relate them together again in a functional (and scriptural) way.

The Son of God stands as head of his body, the church, over all things in creation. The church perpetually exists in him, and does not materialise or become real only when it meets. As we live, work and occupy, we are progressively joining together as members of his body in him. That is why Paul says that the culmination of this age is about 'our gathering together to him' (2 Thes. 2:1). The *ekklesia*, the church, is the body of Jesus Christ. He stands right now in, through, and over the 'all things' of the present creation. Where he is, we are called, as his body, to be together. This unity of the faith is expressed in the way that we live, worship, fellowship, give and, yes, gather. In particular, in line with the creation mandate, this unity of the faith is expressed in our being together as one body in the works we do in creation.

Many leaders are willing to permit a stronger release of the people of God into creation as long as the Sunday gathering and their oversight remains central to the process. They are releasing market-place ministries and kings to conquer the world of work, but are still reserving seats on Sunday and naming the people seated there as 'church central'. Such a controlled release – done in line with an old ecclesiology and in response to a fear that if release is granted, the people might not come back – will not see the church as fullness rise. If the culture affirms the ecclesiastic mother ship as central, dominant and church primary, then, by definition, the rest of what happens will not be any of those things.

By the time this kind of approach to church makes its way out into the world of work, the blaze of affirmation from the central campfire has burned down to a smouldering stub in the hands of the saint. In the darkness all around them, this little light penetrates little darkness. It's hardly surprising that these saints are left pining for the bonfires of the church central to light up their life every Sunday. Hence the need, I believe, to take away a centre that should not have been there in the first place. The church as fullness needs no king, no centre, and no lords to manage it. Jesus is its king and he alone is its centre.

Sounds scary? So it should, because it is. The main reason it is scary is because most leaders do not trust saints to be the church apart from their management of the process. Also, most leaders do not have a theology that can encompass this way of being church. Unless one has a vision and understanding of the church as fullness, the above description will sound like the end of the world. Hence the need to look again at the Hebrew vision and the way of being and building church that arises from it. As leaders, we need to realise that the most pressing issue before us is not so much whether the saints should keep joining with us in our meetings, but how we can get with them in their work. We need to enter into unity with them, not them with us. It is the saints who are in the place where Christ's body, the church, is called to grow up in all things.

Congregational unity – at what cost?

The fear that is often expressed regarding release is that this will scatter the church and thus undermine the unity of the body. To my mind, however, it is the current pattern of church that is working against unity, rather than for it. How so?

Let's say we have a charismatic congregation of 120 members. The leaders and almost all of the people believe in unity, both within their congregation and (more so in the last few years) with the church in the city. Their vision of the church is one that sees the congregation as church proper and primary. They do have cells that meet during the week, and these relate back to the centre for covering, direction and, often, for their teaching content. Their challenge is that two streets away there is a Catholic congregation that would not dream of joining them. Also, three blocks away there is a Baptist meeting that has seven hundred people whom they have never met. Still, they meet monthly with another charismatic group and a Salvation Army corps, and there are plans to get a Methodist congregation to join in. The ministers meet in larger numbers monthly, but after several unity events the congregations have, for the most part, returned to the old status quo. The leaders of this charismatic congregation hope that in five years they will have more unity events, so much so that the church in the city will be able to express that unity to the city and see the results that they have been encouraged to believe will happen when this unity arrives.

So, what's the problem? The leaders' belief that the church is primarily the congregation is the very thing that works to ensure that the unity they are setting out to achieve will not happen. The reason? These leaders set out from the beginning of their church's history to establish unity in their congregation. The reason for this unity is that it produces a stronger congregation. I say this in passing, but it is of note that the real or primary goal of pastors is not so much unity; rather, it is congregation. The building blocks for congregational unity are things like the leader's ministry emphasis, his doctrinal distinctives, his personality and, at the back of these, the history and traditions of the leader's own movement. All of these things work to create an intense and distinct culture within the congregation – one that makes it harder, if not impossible, for other similarly intense congregations to relate or join with them. Each congregation, in line with its doctrine of church, has created such a concentrated, narrow and uniform culture within that it can no longer strongly link to other congregations in the city. In this way, our version of church unity becomes the very thing that works to divide the one church that God sees in each city or territory. Paul has a lot to say about this matter of a divided body in 1 Corinthians 1.

If the charismatic group wanted to really pursue unity in the body, then their own logic would dictate that they stop meeting separately and join, say, with the Catholics. The reason they won't is because they value their own culture of church too highly. They have invested so much energy into their way of church that to forsake it would feel like forsaking the truth itself. The problem is that the same argument is used to support the idea that people should not break into smaller groups with distinct cultures: namely, this would divide the church (as congregation) and lead to elitism. Such an understanding of unity and the logic inherent in it, when applied consistently, is self-defeating. For by defining the church primarily as congregation they have in effect worked to divide themselves from the body of Christ in the city. A denomination leader said to a friend of mine once that he was getting tired of signing unity declarations. He added

'There is more unity happening between the Christian lawyers in the city than in the congregations. While we talk about it, they just do it.' Remember in that accountancy practice the coming together of Catholics, Pentecostals, Baptists and charismatics. Again, it is in relation to our works that the unity of the faith arises. Once relationship through work is established, a meeting of minds and hearts will often follow. The unity is found in and through the work. This unity is not symbolic. It is real: it struggles, it loves, gets angry and loves again. The more this unity grows, the more the people involved will seek to gather in different ways as his body.

I know that I keep turning back to analyse and critique the current form of church. I am aware that many leaders do not entirely fit the bill in terms of what I have outlined. My hope is that pastors won't think I am taking a pot-shot at them as individuals. They work hard, with right motives, to achieve good things for God. Many, if not most, have been responsive to the things that are being said regarding the need for change in our way of being the church. Because of their job, they are more aware of the problem than most. Here, I am going after the thinking that is found, in one form or another, in all of our minds because of Plato and other historical influences. To work through the changes, we need to embrace and to describe what is emerging in the new landscape. We need to contrast and compare it to what is currently in place. Because our thinking forms most of our present structures, to critique these structures is a necessary way of analysing and bringing this thinking out into the open for review and change. The church as construct is not our enemy. As I mention in *Renegotiating the Church Contract*, it is the most tangible expression of who we are and what we think. This is not a 'them against us' scenario. This is about one body, the church, all of us.

Saints need to be given permission to build coordinates, roadways and song lines that do not all have to come from or return back to an ecclesiastic mother ship. They need permission to gather as the church in every place where they are the church. Let's now look at some of the contours that make for the shape of that emerging church.

Pruning meetings so that gatherings grow

We were made to be social creatures, we were made to gather: we can't help it. We don't need too much encouragement to search out people of like mind and soul and spend time with them. This gives me an assurance that if we let go of the current centrist and managed approach to church culture, over time, as the new culture emerges, people will naturally search out ways to gather. They are doing it already in so many ways and in so many places. Again, it's our doctrine of church that causes saints to think that they only really gather as the church when their leaders ordain a meeting time and place for them.

Gatherings are powerful creatures, they accelerate culture like nothing else – both for good and for ill. When a group of people get together and decide to agree on good things, good things happen. When a mob gets together and agrees, bad things are just round the corner. I feel it is important that gatherings of the church as fullness arise as an expression of the culture, rather than coming on line too early in an attempt to generate that culture. Why so?

When a pastor sets out to plant a church, he gathers a group of people together in a room and says 'We are going to build a church.' In that room, for the next however many years, they will meet to worship, fellowship, evangelise, pray, be led, hear preaching and so on. What this does is fix the cultural coordinates for that group of people from then on in. Twenty years on, five hundred people meet in what has now become a larger room. Even though more 'out there' activities might happen, the identity of this large group has from the start been firmly fixed and anchored inside that meeting. The pastor, in a fit of doctrinal frustration, might declare from time to time the need to get 'out there' and win the lost, but the pulpit, the person, the giving and the affirmation that fuels this passion is, as it always has been, 'in here', inside the meeting. Hence the need to not overemphasise the gathering up front. It's a tempting offer, in that to meet is to appear to accelerate the process, but, over time, it will work to limit that culture and work against it.

It is interesting to me that Paul gathered a bunch of people and encouraged them to get together as the church, but did not spend much time talking about that gathering. His main teaching with regard to the gathering was directed at one that was going horribly wrong – that being in Corinth. In the strategy of God for his church taught in Ephesians and Romans the gathering does not feature. One might consider that an exception to this is found in the wrap-up by Paul at the end of Romans, where he sends his greetings to two households in which the church gathered. Here, however, the gatherings are almost an afterthought, a long way from the action detailed throughout these important letters from the apostle. In Ephesians, the book of the church, we find teaching on the standing of the church in creation; there's talk of the divine strategy enacted through our good work; there's teaching about the incarnation and redemption, but nothing about the gathering. I could say that speaking to one another in psalms, hymns and spiritual songs as an alternative to intoxication (Eph. 5:18–19) is one such mention. However, if I tried to create a doctrine from this that the church gathered was the church central, I would be stretching it.

Paul knew that to gather as saints was important. In his letter to Timothy he wrote about how to behave in what he called the household, calling it the pillar and support of truth. However, in his main epistles to the broader body he taught that being church was about life, work, creation and people and not so much about meetings, leaders, preaching and more preaching. Such things as leaders and meetings were in the background, whereas the creation and the works and the saints' engagement of that creation and each other through their works were in the foreground. Paul did not work to build a meeting culture. He set out to build a church that could good-work the earth to the fullness.

We need to follow suit and use Paul's strategy; letting the way that we live, work and relate shape the way that we meet, rather than the other way round. This is done so that the gatherings will be the servant and not the master of the emerging culture. As language, parables, resources and pioneers intensify, the gatherings that emerge will do what gatherings do best. They will express, enrich, intensify and multiply the new landscape culture and be a blessing. They will not, and I hope will never be able to, enclose that culture. Because it did not start in a meeting, it will not end up defined and bound by a meeting.

Creating space to come apart and come together

What happens in relation to gatherings when the church as congregation (or cell) is no longer central and the church as fullness starts to emerge on the landscape? My observation has been that even though people still gathered in Sunday meetings, after twenty years of meetings many had to take a break for a while to locate themselves again. Dangerous? Perhaps, but to my mind not as dangerous as another twenty years of meetings attended by souls who have lost track of themselves along the way. True to human form, these people still talked to other saints, they still had coffee with a friend, and some even began to pray with their spouse. They met, but just didn't have a guitar in their midst when they did.

Many others did not feel the need to stop gathering on Sunday. As an elder, I felt that it was necessary to give people permission to choose, for the first time in a long time, concerning things church. We do it for our children as they grow, so how much more do we need to do it for God's children. I found that once people thought about it and then chose to gather (rather than being expected to just turn up because that's what you did), they were much more present and accounted for than before. Another reason why people did not call for regular gatherings too strongly up front was because the language, parables and resources were still sparse on the ground. In effect, once the initial excitement of doing something new and some debriefing about getting over things old subsided, they did not, at that stage of play, have a lot to talk about.

In our setting, I had to encourage certain people not to rush to meeting mode to fill the quiet spaces of those first years of new landscape life. That's not to say that things were not happening – they were. But you know the drill: seed, ground, die and shoot; then spring, little leaf, small fruit and prune; then autumn, die back, bare branches and the falling leaf dance. It takes a few seasons for an apple seed to be turned into a pie big enough for you to invite friends over for dinner. In our church settings we have become accustomed to showcasing exciting things, either from someone else passing through town or by shining lights on talent, as in music, dance, preaching or drama:

things that can be put on stage and named 'awesome' on a Sunday evening. Works take a lot longer to mature and are not as easily paraded, particularly when they are doing the winter shift.

Of course people will gather in one way or another from the start. Again, that's what people do. There comes a time, however, when the extent of the works, relationships, struggle and fruit is such that people will want to get together more often. As the culture becomes more visible and strong, the people involved will experience a corresponding increase in their desire to pray, learn, fellowship and worship in relation to their experience of church in all of life. It is best that gatherings match the reality that is emerging, rather than pre-empt it by coming on line too soon.

It's not as if I am speaking of some monolithic culture that woke up one morning and said 'I want to meet.' Different people were, as they now still are, doing different things and were at all kinds of places on the map. Some had just discovered the church as fullness and were like reformed smokers giving the old way of church too much stick. Some were getting into their work and discovering God in new ways and were meeting regularly with friends for coffee to talk and pray over what was happening. Three friends met each Thursday for a swim, and then fellowshipped over breakfast to share their struggles and their hopes. Others were taking time out, in recovery mode, getting to know their wife again. Some were watching lots of television. People gathered on Sunday in different fellowships, and appreciated what was on offer there. What I am referring to was more like taking a sounding or doing a litmus test. In the particular setting that I related to, more people were wanting to gather to talk, learn and build more with others in relation to what they had been experiencing. The space that was created was a good thing, in that it caused them to call forth the gathering and, as such, ensured that the gatherings would be theirs and not the leader's responsibility. Let's now take a look at the shape and contours of these gatherings.

14

The Church as Fullness Gathers

James

During the time of the initial growth of the new landscape culture, many people formed for themselves what might be called a composite of being church. As mentors of the developing culture, we had not rushed to declare that this or that new meeting was the new centre around which the culture should orbit and grow. The space created meant that people had time and occasion to locate themselves as the church in different settings. They were no longer under pressure to work out which particular meeting was going to be the centre for their Christian life. As such, they could attend a meeting on Sunday with their family and friends. They could get together with friends for coffee, attend a celebration or a conference, or spend time with a mentor or an accountability group. In all, they were the church, and they had permission to gather as that church. Dangerous? Yes. This is why there is the need for a culture to arise in and through this expression of church, so that sight lines exist to encourage people to have at least three or more people that they identify with more closely and are accountable to. And there is a need to redefine the role of elders and mentors, so that the culture will not be bereft of fathers and mothers.

The truth is, for many ministers this describes their experience of church already. Many find it hard to locate their primary expression of church in their own congregation. The reason for this is that, as a leader, they have a different relationship to the congregation than everybody else has. That's why local church leaders seek out peers to play golf and pray with (or against if they are losing). They attend conferences where colleagues are to be found and they fellowship there. They confide more strongly in their wife than they do in their pastor, because they are the pastor. I say this to indicate that if what I am suggesting is good enough for the goose . . .

I hope I am not sounding over-confident with regard to what might be done. Again, I have written concerning things I saw emerge. As is the case with each person, what I saw was influenced by my convictions on the matter, based on the way that I read Scripture. This interplay between belief and sight is very human, and I confess to having a good dose of it myself. While doing some debriefing, I add here that the most difficult thing for me is the issue I mentioned before concerning when to ebb (back off) and when to flow (hands on). It is hard to know when to more actively initiate or direct things and when to just let things happen. I am not talking about allowing sin to run rampant – this calls for intervention. Rather, I am speaking about the growth of the culture and when and if to throw wood on its fire.

I have friends who are more managerial and tend to set out the plan and follow it through. I have friends who are less enamoured by an organisational approach to reality than I am, who think that *laissez-faire* is a word from the Bible. Often I found that someone would have a great desire to do a work and gather people around it, but then nothing would happen for years. Should I step in and give things a push along? Should I back off and see if the desire is real? Who can tell? My tendency is to wait and see what people really want to do and then, as it starts, add to it. Again, I believe that as ministry gifts we should seek to equip the saints in their works rather than find ourselves, like most ministers in today's church culture, doing most of those works on behalf of the saints. That being said, it's good at times to strongly stir up and dare people to do the good thing that is in their heart. Strong agreement is sometimes the order of the day for people who have not known much of it. No one can know the ideal approach to this, because the ideal doesn't exist. Dancing is a complex and very personal thing. It's best that we learn the steps and then enjoy each other and the music. It's amazing what can happen when you let things happen.

A parable of Scotland

It was on a cold March day that we drove – four Edinburgh professionals in a Jeep – to a building in the middle of nowhere. We took our seats, myself (managing director of a company), the architect, the web designer and the lawyer. Then the preacher began to speak. When he was finished, we drove off frustrated and somewhat angry at the words he had spoken. We were annoyed at ourselves – 'Why didn't I see this before?' – and relieved that now we had an answer to the problem of why the church is so ineffective in evangelism, i.e. if it's not relevant to my life, how can I expect it to be relevant to them? We all could have gone off to grind our axes. But we didn't, because it would have been out of reaction, rather than direction.

We each decided to reflect on what God was saying to us through this and return with a personal vision statement in relation to what we might do next. So we met at my house the next week to review our visions and agree what to do. The theme of the words that rose from this time of reflection was consistent: we each felt our biggest 'crime', over twenty years as Christians, was our lack of connection with each other and our low expectation of what God wanted to do through our work. We decided to meet for friendship and prayer in a café in the centre of town. The café was interesting. It's situated right at the end of the great trade street of Edinburgh and catches a view of the castle that, in the morning, is quite spectacular with the sun behind it. This view inspired me that God was calling us to do something about the city, something relating to governance and eldership, not of church congregations, but of creation.

We started with just the four of us, meeting together and praying for one another at the beginning of the workday. Sometimes we would pray for business or family issues and at other times one of us would rant and get a head of steam up about some issue or other. I remember the strong debate we had in relation to a bill before parliament concerning the promotion of homosexual relationships in schools. The underlying conviction we had was that, as Christians, we had tended to alienate our colleagues, distancing ourselves from them because of our judgmental stances. Contrary to this, Jesus never behaved in this way. He got close to the risky types and very rarely judged them. I have learned that in order to effectively combat the opposite kingdom in someone's life, you have to love the person first and behave in a graceful way towards them. The most powerful spiritual warfare operates in a context of love, not judgement.

The café meetings went on, and we started to gather some lone ranger types who had been following the same theme. We then began to meet in a lawyer's office. This started to gather more momentum. Our times were spent sitting around a boardroom table sharing about life and work issues and praying together. Sometimes we would have a really passionate discussion amongst ourselves. At other times, a particular person would share. After the lawyer's office became too small, we began meeting in a café that opens early at 7.30 a.m. to allow us to do our stuff.

There are probably about forty of us who attend the café now and there could be anything between twenty and twenty-five on any one day. God has brought together a wide range of characters from many walks of life – software designers, a fund manager, a financial analyst, lawyers and pharmacists, health workers and a student who actually gets up early enough to meet with us earthbound people.

The impact of this has been twofold. Firstly, it has allowed us to build relationships and encourage and strengthen each other to reach greater awareness of God operating in our lives. Many stories of prayer being effective – particularly in dealing with conflict at work – have helped us to see how real God's interest is in redeeming the atmosphere that we work in. Secondly, and more importantly, it has given us something of a vision of where we are going. We're definitely on a journey, into something we can't quite see right now. We have to live in the present and strive, work and sweat the Kingdom into our work; but there is something beyond this that is about toppling principalities and seeing a city affected. I believe that we are no longer playing at it any more. In the past month, many of us have been brought to real conflict in work relationships, business difficulty and other trials. But in a sense, these are a welcome test of God's provision and faithfulness. He is right to test our seriousness before we get into more of the battle.

Futures and options

Once the church as fullness has sight of itself and what it is in Christ in creation, there is no end to the diversity we might see. Here are some expressions that I have seen or heard about.

Two friends help facilitate gatherings in the City of London. People are of course busy, so don't often have time to meet for even an hour. So they encourage what they calls 'bands' (drawn from the early Methodists) to meet for around half an hour or so every week or second week. During this time the three or four people (four is generally the limit) cover the bases, which they call 'the three Ps'. Presence: a time for prayer or Bible reading, acknowledging the presence and the power of Jesus in their midst. Pressure: an opportunity to share a pressure that is being faced personally at home or at work. Purpose: seeking the Lord together for God's heart for the City, for the marketplace and for the people they work alongside. This is simply a form, and flexibility is of course encouraged. However, it sets in place a pattern that gives a cultural permission that some would not have the boldness to suggest if it were not there. This link-up of saints also sets the basis for other connections via phone, email or other times of gathering. I include below a part of their statement of intent with regard to these gatherings and their purpose. It is titled 'A call to relationship'.

> The City is an unusual place. It is dynamic and fluid. Its workers form a highly interconnected community. A community that comes together each day with an unusually similar purpose. Its workers share similar pressures and demands. Are those of us who work in the City being called to test pilot a new understanding of Christian community, one that is particularly suited to these special characteristics of the City?
>
> Not a church centred around buildings, but a community centred on relationships.
>
> Not a church built around meetings, but a fellowship built on connections.
>
> Not a church with its own agenda, but a network centred around blessing those who do not yet know Christ.

We do not believe this has to be a weighty task, another responsibility to add to our already impossible schedules. Jesus promises to exchange our heavy burden for his light yoke. The Bible does not make an exception for those who work in the City. We see it as no more of a burden to be part of this community than it is to be with friends.

Will this happen overnight? Probably not. Do we have a right to expect it? No: we have no rights with God, only his grace. Will this definitely happen if we make the right plans? No: God does not respond to a formula. Will success be measured in numbers? No: the Kingdom of God is more intangible than that.

We must learn to walk his way and not ours, to have regard to his priorities, not our own. To learn what it means to wait on the Lord in a city that has no patience. We see a community with no fixed walls, and owned by no one other than Christ. We do not see existing church and fellowship relationships being disturbed. Rather, we see a shared vision woven through existing relationships. Each member of the body delighting in the contribution of others, with unity in diversity and a celebration of the gifts of all. We see no formalised structure to hold this together, only strength of relationships and God's Holy Spirit. It may be untidy, but it will be dynamic.

Another friend of mine who has a background in AA (Alcoholics Anonymous) sees in its traditions, structure and culture many patterns that the church would do well to emulate. AA is known for its Christian origins and use of many Bible principles in its teaching. It has no leadership, no assets and no buildings, but has countless meetings that help millions through their addiction. In many ways, we are all in need of the twelve-step programme. Viewed from any angle, it is a tremendous programme of discipleship. If you get a chance, read the more recent AAderived manual written for Narcotics Anonymous (NA). To meet on common ground, as equals, to share life, face the struggle and agree for the future is what this friend sees as the way ahead for the church. Many I know of could not find honesty in the church, occupied as it was with its own appearance of righteousness, but they found it in an AA meeting, and because of that they forsook sin and found Christ.

Some hold gatherings once a month for four months in the city, which act as a kind of catalyst for the culture. A speaker, some parables, a time to hold a forum around your particular table, then a summary from each table and, finally, time to talk and exchange details, if so desired. After four events this ceases, so that the event itself will not stand out as the main thing.

In line with this, I include here some more news from that brave-heart group of chartered accountants. One of the fellows, from a Catholic tradition, had a vision during a prayer time in the office. He saw the sixth floor of the building they were in purchased by the practice, gutted, fitted and then furnished as a large gathering place. As the group discussed the vision he had seen, their heart for what might be began to take shape. The gatherings would be open for family, friends and clients. There would be no leader, but different people would come, from time to time, to input and teach. There would be no designated worship leader, but different people would come and minister and then others would replace them. One suggestion that I thought was amazing was that if too much momentum started to build, these meetings would be stopped, so that people would not begin to think that they were in any way central to what God was doing.

Another holds something he calls the 'fight club'. It's a man thing, so apologies to the ladies for the exclusivity. No one can speak about the meetings in another setting, except to say that there's one being called for, say, this Friday evening. If someone refers to it and wants to talk about what went on last time, the other person, if they are a member, will look blankly and act as if it does not exist. When a meeting is called, you have to come, no questions asked. They meet in different venues and when they do, the only article of indispensable furniture is a whiteboard with a felt-tipped pen. There is a brief talk to focus things, and then people are invited to write down the things that they have done to wrong God, wrong others and wrong themselves in the past. Honesty is called for, anonymity is demanded. Young men and old write down sins of lust, of pride, of hatred and fear. When the list is done, a prayer for forgiveness and cleansing is declared, and the board is wiped clean. They talk some more and, when the meeting is over, no one is allowed to bring up those sins to another, on pain of being excluded from future meetings (more in-depth counselling is the exception to this rule). Fight club. Exclusive? Certainly! Effective? Absolutely!

There are dinner nights where accomplishments at work are celebrated. One person has just completed an MA, another has had a promotion, someone else has finished a writing project, and a couple are having their fourth child. Time to celebrate what God is doing. Others open their homes as wells rather than cells. These are simply places to come and worship, talk some and go. Little or no teaching is given. They are not held regularly, so as to break the weekly pattern that causes people to turn up because it's Wednesday. They are held to water and refresh the saints who choose to come. Others meet because of a common passion or a desire – Third World debt, micro-enterprise development, government, education – the list of these can be as long and diverse as life itself. There are weekend retreats, where people can spend time talking through the issues of work, spending time with mentors in the business world who can help emerging leaders focus and build in relation to their thinking. Home gatherings that happen every second week, so that friends can note the day and fix it in their diaries. These often meet for a season and then the individuals take a break and decide what might happen next. Also, there are gatherings that revolve around a particular work setting – a health clinic, the accountancy practice and so on. Think again of the extent and diversity of gatherings that happened in Jim Bancroft's factory – discipling meetings in the evenings, fishing, cricket, arts, cycling, bowling, archery and football clubs were as many as Jim could remember.

Once the central congregation lets go of sole ownership of the name 'church', and the fire of that name spreads, it can light up so many places with gatherings of the saints. Each one of these gatherings is no longer in the shadows of the building. They are no longer an extension of the church of elsewhere; they are now populated by people who know they are Christ's body, the church. They know that the church in every sphere and in every territory is one, and has been given one lamp by God (Rev. 2:5). They know that they are that church and have permission to carry its light right into the heart of their life and work in all of creation.

Elders, ministry gifts and other leaders and mentors can work to encourage ways of gathering where good things happen. As is seen in the pastoral epistles of Paul to Timothy, the main motif used of the household gatherings was that of the family. The family motif suggest to us elements that can and should be encouraged in our gatherings: things like belonging, identity in Christ, rights of passage, celebration of special events and days, commitment to the Father and to truth. These, and other things, give people a taste for what life and work are meant to be.

These intensify the culture and, in turn, the culture intensifies them. Again, we are not looking for less from this part of God's provision for our lives, we are looking for more. Let's now add these gatherings to the map.

What about the church on the corner?

Is there a place for the Sunday gathering? Certainly. It may seem that I am against it, but I am not. In our own setting, we have a gathering on Sunday. It used to be central, but now it simply sits as what might be called a more generic (inclusive) event that people can attend if they desire. There is a place for such gatherings, as there is a place for larger celebration events in the city. None of them is the enemy; they are only a problem if we try to make them central. They can sit among the composite of gatherings the saints have access to, and be a blessing to many.

Because we no longer need to load up our church meetings with the visions of pastors, works of ministry, attempts to take the world and so on, we are able to enjoy them all the more. In our own setting, we use the time in our Sunday gathering to worship and share in the Word – and this includes preaching. We endeavour to put on gatherings that reflect and complement the life and work of the people who attend. One of the main ways that we do this is to showcase the various works that people are doing. This can take the form of a narrative spoken by them, or it can be woven into the preaching. If, say, I am talking about heart desire, I will ring up someone during the week who has been following their heart, say, in the healthcare sphere or in childcare, and I will ask them to speak for five minutes about how they relate their desire to their work. This will be my first sermon point, my second will be another person who speaks on their struggle to get through the hard places of work and enact their desire for change. I will comment on this and then lead into a third section of the sermon, where I draw from what has been said and from Scripture, and apply the truth from both to life. This way of showcasing and preaching serves to weave the Word into the life of the saints, while including them in the practice.

For those afraid of a testimony culture boring everybody to tears, there is a simple way to transform a testimony into a sermon. All you have to do is get the testifier to use the word 'you', instead of only using 'me'. 'I found God at work, you can find him too.' 'I worked through this with my boss. You probably have a boss; you can work it through too.' What I endeavour to do is to train people to minister to others from the things that God has done in and through them. I generally introduce them into one of my three-part sermons and then, at the end of that sermon, get them to pray for those who respond. Over time, as they develop, they can take the whole sermon from first joke to last prayer. There is, as mentioned, as much scope as there are good desires and good works in creation.

On our new landscape canvas, the church as construct sits behind a dotted line. The main reason for this is that by taking to itself the rights to be church central and locating itself, for the most part, in its buildings and meetings, it has excluded itself from the setting of the church as fullness. This has caused it to locate itself mostly in buildings and meetings that leaders have called 'church'. Once leaders can see the church as fullness and grasp the theology behind it, they can let the name 'church' go to the saints for their engagement of life and work. As they do this they can, in a seamless way, integrate the gatherings and the initiatives they do with the rest of the life and work of the church as fullness.

It's good to have larger places to gather. It is good to have places in which we can disciple people, not to mention the 'hatch, match and dispatch' work that reaches out to the broader community and serves the saints as well. I am not saying that the cross on top of the building has to come down: some will have a heritage problem with that. Also, others might find it useful to keep, to help them better relate to their immediate community. The matter has more to do with what happens in our hearts, our words, our resource allocation and our gatherings than it has to do with what goes on at the top of our building. Change the culture and embrace the church as fullness and the fixtures and fittings will fall into line as time goes by. Many good works can be done in buildings owned by Christian groups – these were and are never a problem. Again, it's the rights to the centre, it's the management of the Kingdom process, it's the patent on the name 'church' and it's the holding back of the immense resource of ministry gift, gathering, sacrament and permission to the church as fullness that are the problem.

So, don't burn the building. Every space can be redeemed to be a holy space. Whenever a local church congregation wants to surrender its rights to the centre, it no longer marginalises itself, it no longer separates itself from the church as fullness. It is no longer a special or distinct church; rather, the place becomes like any other space made sacred by the power of the saints' agreement, the strengths of the friendship that happens therein and the good work carried out from there. This, after all, is the best of what our church experience is, and this best we want to carry with us into the new. What I have said here is reflected in the following graphic.

Discipling for creation

You may have noticed that I have also added a roadway that finishes as an arrow pointing back up into the graphic. This represents a way of discipleship that we are seeing emerge in the new landscape. The roadway suggests a way of learning that takes place when saints are taken by mentors, elders and/or ministry gifts over the land to learn about Christ, to find out about themselves and to get a taste and sight of the inheritance that their Father God has for them in creation.

We are currently discipling people mostly for congregational life. We need to disciple them for life in creation. Different ministry gifts I know in the new landscape in different nations are working to map out such a journey of discovery for the saints. This includes things like realising with others the heart desires God has created in you; gaining a worldview that enables you to make sense of life; spending time with mentors in the field you are working in; attending several weekends of discussion and training; involvement in a good and redemptive work with others – in all, helping you to be a better disciple of Jesus Christ. This happens over several months or a year, and introduces saints to a culture and network of relationship and the resources therein. Certain people who are setting up apostolic teams to serve the emerging church as fullness (some call them centres, but the word 'team', to my mind, is a safer alternative) are well placed to facilitate things like these.

One more point with regard to this. These journeys of discipleship are such that those who are not Christians are able to join in. We are seeing this in various Christian-led leadership retreat centres and consultancy practices. As people attend a weekend of discussions at a retreat or a seminar given by a saint from the new landscape culture in a business setting, they are drawn by the strength of things like the Hebrew vision of life, the relationships they experience and the quality of input and relevance it has to their life and work. These then ask if there is more that they can access, and can then be invited to join in on the journey. Certain businesses are more able to gather or attract people in this way, particularly those that have an educative component to their work, such as consultancies, retreat centres, schools, health clinics and educational facilities. These are marked on the map by the open hand, like extensions from one of the good-working parables. So ends the graphic. To end this chapter let's go out on a parable with a great name attached.

The Kingsmill Group – a name with providence, a gathering with purpose

The beginnings were very informal, little more than a group of friends whose supper conversations almost always turned to what they liked to think were questions of great moment. As Christians, their abiding concern was how the Gospel of Jesus Christ affected these great questions. Each one of us had a nagging conviction that the Kingdom of God and the government of God in the world were more important than the actions and meetings of the structured church.

In the early eighties, a group began to meet more formally – usually monthly – with a structured agenda and open membership. For each meeting, a clear topic was agreed and one or two people would present a fully researched paper as an introduction to and basis for discussion. Each person attending tried to prepare for the discussion in advance in their own way. Each paper sought to define what the problem was and how the Gospel of Jesus Christ might apply to it and how ordinary Christians might respond in as practical a way as possible. The aim was to develop an understanding of and response to the Kingdom of God in the twentieth century, to try to understand what biblical principles could be brought to bear on real, practical issues and to challenge individual responses accordingly.

The agendas included general and specific questions in economics, education, health, government, justice, poverty, business, the environment, ethics in science, culture and the arts. Increasingly, the agendas expanded to allow individuals to test their own responses to these questions, to re-examine their own lifestyles and to encourage each other in seeing new and practical responses. In particular, the group returned again and again to the question of how Christians respond to the poor. Occasionally, 'experts' were invited to lead the discussion in the area of their expertise.

It would be wrong to suggest that the group itself was solely instrumental in changing individual lives. It was, more likely, one of many influences that at the time converged for this group of people. But many of its members moved, changed or embarked on courses that were significantly different from the conventional career paths in which they had first engaged. They all sought a more challenging call from God.

The following is not exhaustive, but serves to indicate where God took some of the people who gathered as his church to be his church in all of life:

- Setting up the first pregnancy crisis centre in the UK and, subsequently, involvement in CARE.
- Senior economist at the Bank of England.
- From the BBC to the communications department of Tearfund.
- From teaching sociology in a sixth form college to teaching English in universities in the People's Republic of China.
- From headship in state secondary schools in the UK to an international school in South Africa.

- From architecture to opening their family home as a children's home.
- From insurance to Positive Parenting.
- From being a town councillor to an engineer working on overseas development projects.

And why Kingsmill? It was simply the address of the house in which they met.

This is not the church of elsewhere, the church of immense cultural distance from everyday life – it is Christ's body, the church incarnate in the world. These gatherings draw their substance from the work the people do and the relationships they engage in each day. This ensures that these meetings take on the substance of that life and work. They are no longer mostly about the pastor and the vision of the church, they are about where people live and work and relate. As such, these gatherings are able to enrich, clarify, resource and fuel the life and work of those who take part. The church spoken of here is no longer a separate entity that sits on a corner distinct from the saints. The church is now the saints and nothing and no one stands any longer between them. No construct stands between them and God. And no wall stands between them and the creation that holds their inheritance. The culture has birthed the gathering, and because of that, the gathering can serve the culture. The gathering now becomes that which God always intended it to be. It is now the pillar and support to his body, the church, called to be the fullness of him who fills all in all.

15

Order in the City

James

God is a God of order. Hence the need to look very briefly here at the matter of authority and accountability as it pertains to the emergence of the church as fullness. Let's begin by looking at a parable, one that is representative of what is emerging. It's an account from an elder by the name of Nick Pettingale. He is a minister in the city of Burton-upon-Trent, England.

> Historically, here in Burton, there have been levels of unity since the 1980s. This has manifested itself in various forms: prayer breakfasts, family festival weekends and monthly gatherings for church leaders – but nothing like what has taken place recently. About eighteen months ago, as seven leaders met to plan events for the Millennium, eat lunch and pray together, God came – unexpected and unplanned by us! We found ourselves on our knees or faces, weeping and apologising for past arrogance and competitiveness. Critical words spoken and bad attitudes held were confessed and forgiveness was administered.
>
> A kind of covenant took place in our hearts. We agreed to always think the best and to speak well of each other both publicly and privately, to declare from our pulpits that there is only one church in Burton and we are simply a part of it. In the room that day was the local Roman Catholic priest and an

Elim Pentecostal pastor, two Anglican vicars, a 'house church' elder, the Youth for Christ director and myself, a Pioneer Church leader – quite a motley crew! We continue to meet together every two weeks, and every couple of months have a day away together. Those times away together can only be described as awesome, as we prophesy into each other's lives, share Scripture and visions with one another, and support each other through the loneliness of leadership.

Since that time when God came in a special way, we have discovered theology and language that is helping us understand the potential in what God is doing. We now know that the best way to interpret Scripture is in the light of the *one* church in the city; that elders in the New Testament functioned across the city and not in isolated little congregations. Elders primarily sat in a governmental role in the city gates, allowing in that which would bless and forbidding that which would harm the city. We seek to exercise a 'spiritual' authority over the area, the weapons at our disposal being prayer, fasting, holiness and unity, etc. Although we feel it is still very fragile and embryonic, we are experiencing more of the one church in the city than we had previously imagined. We know that we can do more together than we can do apart. We have created a town vision document and, slowly, other church leaders are gathering with us in order to see the town transformed by the Gospel of Jesus.

Because our goal is to transform the city, we are also beginning to engage with Christian politicians, educators, artists, musicians, doctors, etc. We don't call ourselves the 'city elders', because we feel that what is happening needs to emerge more fully over time. Ours is a journey begun, but not yet completed. Our goal is to have the safest streets and the highest school results, the lowest crime and divorce rate and the best pubs and clubs. There will be a town or city in the UK that will be the first to break out in revival – it might as well be ours!

The city gates belong to the elders

As the church as fullness arises, there is much need and much scope for elders to pray, to work and to build together, to see a way of oversight and nurture rise in the city. I don't want to put overmuch in place here that might pre-empt what might emerge. As is the case with the rest of the resources God makes available to us, it is as we reach the place in creation where we need the wisdom, power and glory they contain that we will be able to draw them down from above. Here, a very brief outline sketch is attempted, by way of suggestion and as a contribution to an ongoing discussion regarding order, authority and eldering in the emerging culture.

We know from Scripture that elders exercised their authority in the context of a city. Within that city, many gatherings of saints took place. When elders are no longer located in a managerial position in congregations, they are able to gift the divine capacity for order that God has given them to the church in every sphere of life. They are able to weave divine order into the very fabric of the new landscape culture. They can do this, firstly because it's their God-given calling and, secondly, because they are now in a place of relationship with the saints where it can happen. Elders are able to encourage and help build the culture by offering to the saints the security and parameters they need for growth. What this helps to create is a culture that has what might be called 'internal governance'. This means that divine order is found right through the culture as a value, rather than being placed over it as positional authority.

When elders draw back from running congregations and move to the gates of the city, they are able to establish a power of agreement between themselves that encompasses the entire city – and, by definition, the church therein. Once they realise that they cannot hope to actually be elders over the entire city, or the entire body, they can begin to concentrate on building the kind of culture that brings in the order, the accountability, the richness and health that best expresses the rule of God. Paul uses a term, in 1 Timothy 2:1–2, which speaks to us of the kind of culture in view here. He urges that 'entreaties and prayers, petitions and thanksgivings, be made on behalf of all men, for kings and all who are in authority'. These prayers and the people who pray them work, over time, to help bring about an environment where the body is able to live a 'quiet life in all godliness and dignity'. Sounds to me like a great culture in which to bring up children, work, and shine light! Elders who are acting as managers of congregations can't do this. Even when they draw back to the city gates, there are only a few people that each of them can directly relate to. The only way that their roles as elders can be expressed is if they work to bring about a culture that can carry and express the 'quiet life in all godliness'. As is the case in any good family, elders are meant to establish stronger initial parameters for the saints, which progressively move out to permit more space for ongoing development and good culture to arise.

This way of exercising eldership is done by relationship. It is carried by relationship and it is kept going by relationship. Again, we need to remind ourselves that the things we are looking to see emerge are not something we have to manufacture out of nothing. We are simply looking at drawing out the reality that God himself has put there in creation. What I am saying is that it's not as hard as it looks! The elders who meet in Burton simply established an agreement between themselves, prayed, related, and left the door open for others to come through. From there, the things that God has in store for those who love him in Burton began, and will continue, to emerge. One very important development, that it would be good to note here, is the way in which these elders began to invite people involved in different fields of work to join in fellowship and, from there, to take an eldership role in the city with them. In this way, they began to extend their power of agreement with people who were representative of the different spheres of work in the city. In turn, these people could then better express that authority and eldership in their spheres of work and relationships.

'Mentor' is a good word. These kinds of people, as we know, have experience, wisdom and a desire to work with others to help them find their place in life and work. Elders can work with mentors in various work spheres to encourage and resource them to come alongside saints working in those spheres. Just as a ministry gift works with apostolic individuals to encourage them to break ground in their particular field, elders need to pass on as much as they can of their gift and anointing to faithful others. The many benefits of this are obvious. In particular, it helps create an environment where eldership can happen in the place where people live and work. This mentoring and peer support needs to go hand in hand with a culture that encourages people to be in relationships of accountability with at least two or three people. This serves to create a culture where people are not lone rangers, living as a law unto themselves. We are looking here, again, at more of a composite of accountability being developed by people – one that can encompass every sphere of their life and work.

Remember those business people who were driven to succeed because they did not have permission to be who they are from their fathers? So many sons and daughters work without the power of agreement in their life. They are in need of someone to carry the permission and agreement of the Father in heaven to them on earth. Elders cannot do this of themselves, but a culture of agreement, one that is expressed by mentors and peers who extend trust and support, can. These business people did not want success, they wanted permission to live and be loved – ultimately by their Father God. We need to plant the Father's permission deep into the heart and relationships of the saints. As we do, we will progressively see great and good works emerge from the permissioned nature of every one of his sons and daughters.

When a broad culture is in place, a much greater opportunity exists to encourage good decisions and good actions that safeguard against problem behaviour. If leaders simply released saints and did not work to build the culture, there would indeed be a problem. They, however, would be the ones accountable for that, as leaders, rather than the saints being primarily liable for the disarray that would ensue. If, however, a good consensus culture was in place, one agreed upon by one's peers and mentors, if something dysfunctional started to happen it could be dealt with much sooner. The more we actively build the new landscape culture, the stronger the relationships, the order and the eldership will be. The more these relationships are built, and the more his body, the church, is released, the greater, I believe, will be our response to, our exercise of, and our understanding of divine order and authority in creation.

If I were to include elders in the graphic, I would put a few of them around the map with large hearts and good eyes. If, however, I did, I would perhaps give the impression that authority was something only a few select people possessed. Ultimately, the value, gift and strength of elders are manifest as their qualities become intrinsic to the culture. This brings in a strong and divine internal governance to the church as fullness. This is akin to the divine order God brought in during the time of Judges: a time when Israel had no king except God. The nation was well served by God-given prophets, judges and elders of tribes. Of course, there were many problems, but these were not solved by the installation of a king. In truth, even though there were some good kings, the rule from the centre created more problems than it solved. If I were to complete the graphic of the new landscape church, I would prefer to see authority, accountability and eldership portrayed as part of the entire fabric of that landscape. Then I would finish the drawing by declaring again that Jesus Christ, the head of his body, the church, is to be found in, through and over this entire landscape. I could paint him in, but I would prefer to leave that to you.

16

Whoever Gets the Name 'Church' Wins

David

There is a battle on as you finish this book. This is not some clever, avant-garde theology; this is truth coming up against a mindset, a stronghold if you will. Earlier in the book we saw it as a virus. What's at stake is not some cheap game of point-scoring in the latest and most provocative messages. What's at stake is the future of God's people in this generation. There was a powerful moment in the life of Peter when a revelation dawned. The Messiah turned to him and said these words: 'On this rock I will build my church, and the gates of Hades will not overcome it. I will give you the keys of the kingdom of heaven; whatever you bind on earth will be bound in heaven, and whatever you loose on earth will be loosed in heaven' (Mt. 16:18–19).

All kinds of interpretation have been offered for this passage, but there are some obvious points to make. It is surely less than credible to suggest that the gates of Hades are interested in gatherings as their primary sphere of warfare. Something more expansive, more relevant, more vital is at stake here. The church is set in the context of the Kingdom – the rule of God through all creation – earth and heavens. The Kingdom, in itself, offers the keys to all of earth and heaven. It is the overarching link between the two realms, and the church is the agent by which those keys turn, to open or shut, to release or to bind.

This is powerful, heady stuff, with cosmic implications. One dare not suggest that the gathering can, or should attempt to, achieve all of this. If the church is not the gathering then that which carries its name carries immense cosmic significance. The church is not the gathering, the church is the body of Christ living and working in every sphere of life. The heart of every believer knows that, and we long for it to emerge. The enemy knows it full well and will try his level best to obscure the issues and confuse the searchers. But he can't win: the gathered ones know there is something afoot. Their wax-blocked, meeting-covered ears are hearing the faint but unmistakable sounds of the royal trumpet. Something is stirring, and the body of Christ – designed to be the fullness of him who fills all in all – is beginning to stir from her virus-induced, comatose sleep.

The wake-up call

I love the times I have with my kids – even now that they are grown up – when I go into their rooms to make sure that they are awake or get them to wake up. Every day it's different. Sometimes their sleepy eyes engage mine, and they plead for more time. At other times they move faster to complete a school assignment or get ready for work. I remember a friend taking one of our sons birdwatching early in the morning. At 4 a.m. he called my son, who jumped out of bed instantly and walked straight downstairs, ready and alert, desperate not to miss any of the adventure that was waiting for him. It's different for each one and it's different each day. I shake them, call them, sometimes even tickle them, to get them ready for the new day.

Someone asked me recently 'What has been the impact on you of this outpouring of God's Spirit?' It took me a while to answer, as I thought through the implications of the last number of years. Finally I said 'It has been a wake-up call.' I realised then that something from deep within me had responded to heaven's voice. The emotional and spiritual highs had served as a prelude to a wake-up call that was now stirring the very recesses of my being. These past years, reader, God has been calling you and me, shaking us and sometimes tickling us to wake us up to the sound that's now coming from heaven. Some have already jumped up alert and ready to go – others are lying still, pleading for more time in the old.

In a recent vision, a friend of mine saw the church surrounded by clocks ticking and tocking away: time was being spent on gathering, on programmes, on activities. It was now time for the alarms to ring; time for the wake-up call. She saw a stairway leading up to a wide open door, and through the open door was a new landscape. To the left were lots of buildings, some tall; to the right were green fields with lots of people. A voice was saying 'It's time to take the first step.'

Hide and seek – God's game in his new landscape

I know God loves hide and seek. In Proverbs it says that it is the glory of God to conceal things and the glory of kings to search them out. The Song of Solomon has often been quoted during these past six years. In this book the bride is represented as constantly searching for her lover. If you will, it is an erotic game of hide and seek. In chapter 5:6–8 she says, 'I opened for my lover, but my lover had left; he was gone. My heart sank at his departure. I looked for him but did not find him. I called him but he did not answer.' Many of you reading this right now can mirror those words – you know the story. But here is my question for you: Where did the beloved find her lover? She found him in the streets and squares of the city (3:2) – in the places of everyday life and work.

It's time, saints! Three times in the book it says 'Do not awaken love until it so desires'. In these recent years a new love has been awakened. There is an unstoppable hunger in God's people, the church. We will no longer find our lover primarily in the church meeting. And when we do, I believe that for the most part it will be as he thrusts his hand through the latch-opening, calling us out by making our hearts pound for more of him. And when we open for our lover we will discover that he has gone into the city. Reader, like the river heading for the sea, our lover has gone and he will be found by those who look for him, not primarily in the gathering but in all of life and work.

It's time for leaders

> 'I foresee a change in doing church, where church supports its workers, not the workers the church.'(Dave Richards)

> 'In nothing has the church so lost her hold on reality as in her failure to understand and respect the secular vocation. She has allowed work and religion to become separate departments and is astonished to find that as a result, the secular work of the world is turned to purely destructive and selfish ends and that the greater part of the world's intelligent workers have become irreligious or at least uninterested in religion. But is it so astonishing? How can anyone remain interested in a religion which seems to have no concern with nine tenths of his life?'(*Creed or Chaos*, Dorothy L. Sayers)

It is time for us as church leaders to hear the voice and settle the issue. Church programmes, meetings and activities are not meant to be a parasite, sucking into themselves all the most able, most qualified and most spiritual. Church leaders need to equip those individuals and fling them out into every sphere of service, work and activity, 'equipping the saints for the work of service'. We should not hold all the best to ourselves: we are freely to give our best, and then follow them into every sphere of service that God has called them into.

By our words, actions and priorities we set out to make working men and women see as we see, feel as we feel and speak as we speak. Commitment then is not from us to them but from them to us. We say the church is not a building. We say the church is not meetings; but look for a moment at the language of our commitment courses. We ask for their commitment to tithe and attend the meetings we put on. Our language tells us what we really believe. How about a commitment course where the leadership team affirms the unique and high calling of the individual to their work sphere? What would happen if the leadership team committed themselves to equip every member for the works of service to which they were called by God? Imagine a community where each member committed themselves not to church meetings but to living out the Kingdom of God in all of life and work; where church leaders and elders designed gatherings to meet the needs, fuel the vision and equip the ministers and priests for their works of service in all of creation.

I was working with my friend and mentor Dave Richards last year in a Kenyan city. We had preached these words to around twelve thousand people during the course of a week. On the last night, I asked the two thousand or so assembled 'How many here are full-time for the Lord?' First time, the pastor's hand and one or two others went up. After four or five times of asking, perhaps twenty hands in total went up: twenty out of two thousand – just one per cent! That tells us what the others really believed. The Christian caste system wants to put its special mark on the forehead of just the few, and in this case it had been very successful. To crush this serpent, leaders, it must start with you and me.

I'm not knocking those who live off the Gospel. All over the world many of you leaders reading this material have made serious sacrifices. You have left a job or career to focus on what you believe God has called you to do. I want to honour you here and thank you from the bottom of my heart. Most of my closest friends are those who live off the Gospel, and they, more than any others, are the ones who have encouraged me to speak and write as I have done here. For their sake, and for the sake of millions of saints around the world imprisoned by the theology of second best, I want to say loud and clear: let's give the name 'full-time' to all God's people. It needs to be said again and again, until a stronghold is broken and the heel of the church at work crushes the Christian caste system. This stronghold is powerful and, like the creeping weed varieties in my garden, regularly needs to be uprooted.

What a difference it would make to so many Christians to be released into confident ministry right where they are. Nehemiah, Joseph, the Exodus midwives, Naaman's servant girl, Daniel, Esther, Lydia would all have approved. Does God really differentiate between Daniel and Elijah, between Joseph and Samuel, Abraham and Nathan? Does he differentiate between Amos and Eli, between Peter and working Paul, between the apostle John and Prisca and Aquila? On whose forehead would you dare to place the special mark? If you want to follow a biblical analogy then surely, with regard to the New Testament teaching, we would agree that we are a kingdom of priests - that's all of us. As leaders, we have taught from our earliest days the priesthood of all believers – let's not recant when the going gets tough and the way ahead becomes costly.

The Prince of Life is kissing ready lips and the ruler's bride is waking up. As her beautiful form rises to fill all of creation, what will our church leaders say and do? For centuries they have been paid from the royal treasury and have, for the most part, been nursing, grooming and preaching to the court. I don't doubt that they are faithful, hardworking, godly, sacrificial men and women. But as the court changes and the bride leaves the building, running in her new-found freedom, what will they do?

In their shock, will they let her go so far, then pull her back because they know no other way? Will they fret and worry about losing what for so long they have held? Will they worry that they will lose all they thought they had? Will they worry that their role will be less valued or that the voice they heard so long ago calling them to ministry in the church was false? Or will they run to keep up with the bride? Will they serve her on the move? Will they see new horizons of ministry unfold in spectacularly unpredictable ways? Will they see this time as more or less? Will their hearts swell in anticipation or shrink back in fear? I don't know, but the choice is there for each one of us.

Pastors and leaders, are you scared of release? Maybe you are asking the question 'Will the people return, if I release them and let them find their way as the church in all of life and work?' It is not a matter of releasing them and thinking that's that. It's a matter of going with them, equipping them, agreeing with them, serving them with language and affirmation in their engagement of the spheres of creation. As we said, for those with eyes to see, there is not less work, there is more.

Could we, as leaders, serve these Kingdom priests as they nervously, haltingly, engage in their new-found freedom and responsibility? And if we get afraid that they may not come back, let's remember the many times we have sent people out to the mission field in other nations. Didn't God bless and reward every single time by sending others to us? I have faith that the same will be true with our new mission field for all of God's people.

As the mustard seed grows into the tree, let's not make it into a bonsai. Let's not start clipping away at its roots, buds and branches by continually focusing in on our gatherings. Of all the generations that have lived on the planet we have surely been most blessed. Blessed with teaching, blessed with the Holy Spirit, blessed with resources. Will we see this window of opportunity and change our thinking, change our church structure and release our church people to fulfil the high calling of God at work?

It's time for saints

Saints, in every sphere of paid and unpaid work, are you ready to follow Jesus to the workplace? Are you ready to take the plunge into the sea of God's adventure, not even sure you can swim well enough, long enough or in the right direction, but following his voice because you've heard it?

Saints, will we be the church that works? The time is now; the opportunity of a millennium lies before us. As the clocks of church gathering and church programmes tick away around us, it's time to climb the stairs to the open door that stands before us. Through that open door stands a new landscape waiting for your arrival, your participation, your heart. If not you and me, reader, then who else?

I know that in these last few years of hopes raised and deepening disappointments, God has been preparing all of his people for exactly such a time as this. Even as I write this, and as you read this, there is a tug in our minds and our hearts. He's speaking to us and we know it.

There's a glory to fill all the earth and it's in you. There are good works with angels and light embedded in their unfolding; works pre-ordained and waiting for you. There are works of service for which he has been equipping you and no one else. The fullness of him who fills all in all is waiting for your fullness to complete his purposes on the earth. Be free: fly like the eagle you are.

Where to now?

Congratulations for getting this far! Continue to weigh the message in this book and judge it, and if you know it's God speaking to you, then it's over to you to make your response. There is no clear six-step programme to follow. If this truth is Spirit-born, the wind will move those who respond where he wants. So, hoisting the sail and moving with him is our best response. How do we do that? I can't tell you exactly, but I can point in the direction of the start line.

Saints, this book is not a call for you to jettison your fellowship and stop gathering. The challenge is to sit down with the ministry gifts that God in his providence has placed around you and to dialogue and pray through the implications. From there let saints and leaders alike affirm, encourage, release and push each other out of the nest and into creation.

Leaders, if you want to see the key of the Kingdom turn in your congregation, call the saints up to be the church at work and release them with no strings attached into the new landscape. Release them with the power of agreement that guarantees the response of their Father in heaven. I urge you: please affirm, encourage and serve the saints with all the resources God has given you. I know that some will find this frightening, some radical, and others will find it exciting. But whatever the emotion, could we just do it? The power of release is in our hands and our mouths. Let's open our hands and speak the words with faith, a smile and a releasing spirit.

Leaders and saints alike, let's not shrink back into the sweaty duvet, musty from centuries of sleep. Let's wake up and run through the open door. Let's run to find our lover God waiting on Monday as on every other day to welcome his church at work.

Appendix I

References

Chapter 1
Acts 7; Hebrews 11; Daniel 1:3–20.

Chapter 2
Ezekiel 47:6–12.

Chapter 3
Matthew 16:18, 5:16

Chapter 4
Colossians 1:23; 2 Corinthians 12:2; Romans 1:20; Ephesians 4:6, 4:9–10, 1:20–23; Isaiah 66:1; Ephesians 5:2, 5:3, 4:15, 6:12, 5:21–33, 6:5–9, 4:15, 4:13; 1 Timothy 3:15; John 14:6; 1 Peter 2:9.

Chapter 5
Romans 13:6.

Chapter 6
Genesis 1:1, 1:2, 1:27, 1:28, 2:3, 2:15, 2:18, 2:19, 3:17–19; Philippians 2:13; Exodus 35; Psalm 103, 104; Micah 4:3; Galatians 3:28; 1 Thessalonians 4:11–12; Colossians 3:22–25, 4:1–2; Ecclesiastes 3:22; Romans 12:1

Habakkuk 2:14; Ephesians 1:23, 2:10, 4:6, 4:11–12, 6:13f; Matthew 5:16; Hebrews 1:14.

Chapter 7
Ephesians 4:11.

Chapter 8
Matthew 18:18–20; 2 Thessalonians 1:11–12; Romans 6:1.

Chapter 9
Colossians 1:23; John 7:17, 16:29–30; Ephesians 4:15; Matthew 13:35.

Chapter 10
Colossians 1:10; Ephesians 4:15.

Chapter 11
Ephesians 4:8–13; Matthew 24:45; Revelation 19:10.

Chapter 12
1 Corinthians 3:10; Ephesians 4:16; Colossians 1:9–10; Ephesians 2:15; 2 Timothy 2:2.

Chapter 13
Philemon 1:2; Romans 16:3–5; 1 Timothy 3:15; 1 Corinthians 1:12; 2 Thessalonians 2:1; Ephesians 5:18–19.

Chapter 14
Revelation 2:5.

Chapter 15
1 Timothy 2:1–2.

Chapter 16
Matthew 16:18–19; Song of Songs 5:6–8, 3:2

Appendix II

Bibliography

Chapter 1
Marshall, Rich, *God@Work*, Shippensburg, Destiny Image Publishers Inc., 2000

Chapter 2
Daily Telegraph, 1 May 2001

Chapter 4
Oliver, David, *Work – Prison or Place of Destiny?* Milton Keynes, Word Publishing, 1999

Chapter 6
Thwaites, James, *The Church Beyond the Congregation*, Carlisle, Paternoster, 1999

Chapter 6
Temple, Archbishop William, *Towards the Conversion of England*, out of print

Chapter 15
Sayers, Dorothy L., *Creed or Chaos*, Manchester, USA, Sophia Institute Press, 1949, 1974